W9-AHZ-178

WHEELS!

WHEELS!

the
KIDS'
BIKE BOOK

MEGAN STINE

A *Sports Illustrated For Kids* Book

39065
J
796.6
STI

Copyright © 1990 by The Time Inc. Magazine Company

All rights reserved. No part of this book may be reproduced in any form or by any electronic or mechanical means, including information storage and retrieval systems, without permission in writing from the publisher, except by a reviewer who may quote brief passages in a review.

First Edition

Library of Congress Cataloging-in-Publication Data

Stine, Megan.
    Wheels!: the kids' bike book / by Megan Stine —1st ed.

        p. cm.
    "A Sports illustrated for kids book."
    Summary: Discusses choosing a bike, equipment, accessories, instructions for riding, and customizing.
    ISBN 0-316-81625-6 (hc)
    ISBN 0-316-81624-8 (pb)
    1. Cycling—Juvenile literature. 2. Bicycles—Juvenile literature.   [1. Bicycles and bicycling.] I. Title.
                        Title: Kids' bike book.
GV1043.5.S75   1990
796.6—dc20   89-29661
                                                         CIP
                                                          AC

SPORTS ILLUSTRATED FOR KIDS is a trademark of THE TIME INC. MAGAZINE COMPANY.

Sports Illustrated For Kids Books is a joint imprint of Little, Brown and Company and Warner Juvenile Books. This title is published in arrangement with Cloverdale Press Inc.

10 9 8 7 6 5 4 3 2 1
RAI

For further information regarding this title, contact Little, Brown and Company, 34 Beacon Street, Boston, MA 02108

Published simultaneously in Canada
by Little, Brown & Company (Canada) Limited

Printed in the United States of America

Illustrations by Jackie Aher
Interior Design by Bob Feldgus

This book is dedicated to Betty Miller
for her talent, courage, grace and optimism.

ACKNOWLEDGEMENTS

Special thanks are due to Beau Jones of Atlanta, Georgia, for his advice, technical expertise and enthusiastic insight into the world of cycling. The author would also like to thank the following people who helped prepare this book: Jim Fremont, Education Director of the Bicycle Federation of America; Patrick Renau of Sportstown, Atlanta; Peter Trewin; and Dee Rambeau and Mike Swartz of the American Bicycle Association.

CONTENTS

Chapter 1 FINDING THE RIGHT BIKE   **2**
From mountain bikes to road racers—everything you need to know to choose the bike that's perfect for you.

Extra! **Bike Talk**   **11**

Chapter 2 IT'S A FRAME-UP!   **12**
Taking the mystery out of the important parts of your bike: the frame, brakes and gears.

Extra! **Cycle Search Game**   **19**

Chapter 3 RIDING! TIPS & TECHNIQUES   **20**
The secrets of shifting gears, braking, cornering and more.

Extra! **Trivia Match Game**   **27**

Chapter 4 GET INTO GEAR!   **28**
What's necessary and what's fun—all the hottest bike gear.

Chapter 5 WILD WHEELS!   **35**
Some of the strangest cycles ever built—and the people who rode them!

Chapter 6 TUNE-UPS & TOTAL REPAIRS   **47**
How to fix your bike and keep it running like a dream.

Extra! **Show-Off Smart-Off Quiz**   **52**

Chapter 7 RIDE ACROSS AMERICA   **53**
See the USA—on your bicycle! With special tips for touring and training.

Extra! **Bicycling's Best, The Record- Breakers**   **60**

Chapter 8 THE RACE IS ON!   **61**
From the very first races to races you can enter yourself—this is cycling at top speed!

Glossary   **73**

MORE ABOUT BICYCLING   **75**

ANSWERS TO QUIZZES AND PUZZLES   **79**

WHEELS!

INTRODUCTION

Biking! If there's one thing that almost every kid in America likes to do, it's ride a bike. Hopping on a bike and zooming down the street on a warm summer afternoon with the breeze blowing through your hair is fantastic! You can use your bike for fun, for sport and for transportation. Ride it to school, use it on your paper route, race against your best friends or go on an errand for your dad. You can do stunts on a BMX bike or just go for a ride to get out of the house. Riding a bike means being able to go places on your own. In other words, it means freedom!

But here's a weird piece of bicycle trivia for you. Did you know that in the 1800s when bicycles were first invented, they were ridden by adults—not kids? It's true. The first bikes were considered adult toys, too large and too difficult for kids to ride. Only young, strong men could ride the Velocipede or the Ordinary, as the early high-wheeler bikes were called. It wasn't until bicycles got smaller, in the early twentieth century, that kids were allowed to ride them. When automobiles came along, adults gave up riding bikes, and bicycles became a "For Kids Only" thing.

These days, biking is for everyone. And there's a bike for every experience. There are even bikes made to ride in the snow! So grab a helmet, climb on your bike and let's go! The streets may be crowded, but there's still room for one more—and it ought to be you!

FINDING THE RIGHT BIKE

Imagine that your birthday is coming up soon, and what you want more than anything in the world is a new bike. You've been telling your parents for weeks that you absolutely have to have a new bike, but you're not sure they're really listening. So you sit down and write them a reminder note.

Dear Mom and Dad,

Don't forget: I want a bike for my birthday!

Love,

Your Excellent Son or Daughter

Now, what's wrong with that letter?

You don't have to be a genius to see the problem. The letter doesn't tell Mom and Dad what *kind* of bike you want. Just think how miserable you'd be if they bought you a racing bike when what you really wanted was an off-road mountain bike. Or the other way around.

Maybe you don't even know what kind of bike you want. There seem to be a zillion choices, so many different makes and models that it can make your *head* spin, let alone your tires! Mountain bikes, racing bikes, touring bikes, BMX bikes, city bikes and more. Each bike is made for specific kinds of riding conditions, and it can't be used in others. You can't take a racing bike on a mountain trail and expect it to do well. And you won't win any road races on a standard mountain bike, either. So the trick is to find the bike that's right for you.

There aren't as many choices for kids' bikes as there are for teenagers' and adults'. *Most* kids' bikes come with fat tires, upright handlebars and no gears. But not all of them. If you want to shift gears, you can find 3-speeds, 5-speeds, 10-speeds, even 12-speed bikes made for kids. You'll also have a choice of hand brakes or coaster brakes (the ones that stop the bike when you pedal backwards). And you'll have a choice of colors and trim.

Before you go out and buy a bike, you need to find out what different bikes can do and what the different kinds of bikes are called. Depending on where you live, there can be two or three different names for the same thing. Whatever kind you choose, you'll also need to make sure the bike fits your body.

If you'd like to learn about the bike's body—the frame and parts—you should read Chapter 2. And if there are any names or terms you're unsure of, check the Glossary in the back of the book. Whether you're buying your first bicycle or moving on to a bigger and better one, you'll be better off if you know something about bikes

WHEEL FACTS

- **Mountain bikes were invented by cyclists who wanted to ride up Mt. Tamalpais in Marin County, California. Most recent bicycling trends have started in California, where cycling is a year-round sport. BMX racing and stunts also originated there.**

before you hit the stores. Here are the major kinds of bikes you'll find:

KIDS' BIKES

You'll find that most bikes made for kids come in one of these two styles:

MOUNTAIN BIKES

These bikes are also called off-road bikes or ATBs, which stands for All Terrain Bikes. With their fat, knobby tires and straight, upright handlebars, mountain bikes have become one of the most popular styles of bike in recent years. True mountain bikes are rugged enough to be ridden on rough mountain trails, and they have a sophisticated gear system to help you climb hills like a mountain goat. On a good ATB, there may be as many as 21 gears. The frames are very hard to break, and mountain bikes are very comfortable on the road. The fat tires give you a more "cushy" ride, and the upright handlebars make it easy to look around while you're riding.

But don't be fooled! Many bikes sold for kids might look like mountain bikes because of the fat tires—but they're not really strong enough for all-terrain riding. On a lower-priced bike, especially bikes sold in discount stores, the wheels may not be sturdy enough to ride over rocky ground, and the brakes are not strong enough to stop you when you're zooming down a dirt hill. Also, you usually don't get gears until you buy the largest size kids' bike with 24-inch wheels.

Some of the better quality 20-inch bikes look like ATBs, and even though they really aren't,

they're still good bikes. They're well made, with strong frames and good features—and if that's what you're looking for, great. Just remember that you can ride these ATB look-alikes on some terrains, but not all. They are fine on grassy fields but not on steep trails, for instance. Ask your dealer to be honest with you about how much rough riding your bike can take.

If riding in the wilderness or getting off the road seem like the ultimate in fun, then the action-packed thrill of mountain biking could be for you!

BMX BIKES

Fat, knobby tires…upright handlebars…tough frames…hey, wait a minute! This sounds like a mountain bike all over again! What's going on?

Sure, BMX bikes do look something like mountain bikes. But there are two big differences. Number one: BMX bikes are almost always one-speeds. Unlike mountain bikes, BMX bikes have no gears to shift. The second difference is that the true BMX bikes never have wire spokes on the wheels.

BMX means "bicycle motocross," which is a kind of racing. (Get it? B for bicycle, M for moto, and the X stands for cross.) Motocross racing was originally motorcycle cross-country racing, but today it means something else. It's a specialized kind of race held on a dirt track, and it includes wild jumps over small dirt hills—*bam!* The landings are tough. In a BMX race the rider almost never sits down!

There are also freestyle BMX competitions which involve jumps and turns in midair. In order to take that kind of shock, a BMX bike must be super-sturdy. The best ones are built with heavy steel tubing and reinforced welded joints. The front fork on a good BMX bike will be much thicker and heavier than those on other styles of bikes because that's where a lot of the impact goes. And there will be a *double* stabilizer bar instead of a single top tube. All true BMX bikes—even the ones ridden by adults in competitions—have 20-inch wheels.

Other BMX features include tube padding, hand-operated brakes and mag wheels, which have five thick molded plastic spokes instead of many wire spokes. You can also get retractable

For a radical ride, try a BMX bike!

"stunt" pegs—small, stiff arms which flip down from the fork so you can stand near the front wheel. You can learn to do tricks while standing on the pegs. These stunts are one of the most exciting parts of freestyle competition. Some BMX freestyle bikes also have a completely free-spinning handlebar. Instead of turning only partway to the left or right, these handlebars actually spin in a complete circle, 360 degrees, and allow the riders to do even more tricks.

Some BMX bikes come with longer cranks (the part of the bike that holds the pedal). Some riders think a longer crank helps your foot to stay on the pedal. Other people say the longer crank slows you down by hitting the ground when you're going around a sharp turn. If you're looking for a BMX bike to use in competition, tell the dealer

that's what you're looking for. Be sure to get a heavy-duty machine and check out the cranks carefully.

Most 20-inch and smaller bikes sold for kids are BMX look-alike bikes. In other words, if you're buying a 20-inch bike, it's likely you'll end up with a BMX style. But again, don't think that just because a bike is called a BMX, it's strong enough to take a pounding. Wheelies and high-flying jumps are dangerous enough on a good bike. On a flimsy, inexpensive bike, something's going to get damaged and it might be *you*!

One final warning: Some BMX-style bikes come with very high "ram's horn" handlebars. Avoid the tallest ones. These high-rise handlebars can be very dangerous during a fall—and they don't allow you as much control of your bike either.

FOR GIRLS ONLY

Were girls' bikes developed because girls *couldn't* ride a boys' bike for some reason? Or did it have anything to do with girls' bodies? No. It was mainly the problem with skirts and looking ladylike—nothing more.

In the old, old days, when bicycles were first invented, women never wore jeans or pants. It just wasn't considered ladylike! So girls' bikes had to be designed differently, to allow women to get on and off gracefully. Hop on a boys' bike—sometimes now called a standard bike—wearing a dress or skirt, and you'll see what we mean. You can't throw your leg over the top tube very easily while wearing a skirt.

Skirts aren't a problem anymore. These days, most women prefer to wear pants or, better yet, cycling shorts while riding. But there is another reason why girls sometimes still prefer a girls' bike. Size! Since girls are often shorter than boys, it can be hard for a girl to straddle a boys' bike. (See "All About Bike Sizes" later in this chapter.)

Do you want to buy a girls' bike? The choice is up to you. You might like the fact that on a girls' bike, you can simply step "through" the opening in the frame and then climb on the bike. Then again, since very few adult bikes are made with a girls' frame, you might buy a standard frame with a top tube, so that you can get used to swinging your leg over right from the start. That way, when you move up to an adult bike, you'll have more bikes to choose from and won't have to get used to a whole new style. No matter what you decide, one thing is for sure: If you want a pink bike with white hearts painted on the frame, you'll probably have to go for a girls'-style frame.

The traditional girls' bike has no top tube—or rather, the top tube is angled down and attached at a lower point on the seat tube.

Bigger Bikes

The rest of the bikes in this chapter aren't made in kids' sizes. But if you're about five feet tall or taller, your next bike will probably be an "adult" bike, and you may want to buy one of these.

ROAD OR TOURING BIKES

In the old days they used to be called 10-speed bikes. Now, forget it! There are 10-speeds, 12-speeds, 14-speeds, 15-speeds, 16-speeds and 18-speeds—and by the time you read this, there may be 48-speeds! Currently the 12-speed is the most common. No matter how many gears they have, however, road bikes all have three things in common. They have thin, smooth tires; lightweight frames; and down-curved handlebars. All of those features are designed to make the bike lightning quick, which is why some people call these bikes "racing bikes." They are also called touring bikes, and bicycle manufacturers call them lightweight bikes.

Road bikes are meant to be ridden on pavement, never on grass or turf. They're great for long-distance riding, or touring, because the lightweight frame makes them easier to ride without getting tired. The dropped handlebars, however, force the rider into a low, bent-over position—a streamlined position which cuts down on wind resistance but is slightly less comfortable for the rider.

As for how many gears you'll need, that depends on how much you ride and in what kind of landscape. A good gear system helps you ride up steep hills without huffing and puffing the whole way. If you live some place flat, like Kansas, you probably don't need 15 gears. In San Francisco, on the other hand, you'll want to go for as many gears as you can afford! In general you'll find that the bikes with more than 12 gears are slightly heavier, and the extra weight will slow you down. So don't choose a bike with lots of gears just to be cool. Try to figure out how much hilly riding you'll be doing, and then pick a bike that's right for you. If you're not tall enough for a real road bike, don't give up. In the meantime you can cruise the streets on a 10-speed and still achieve awesome speeds.

CITY BIKES OR CROSSOVER BIKES

Sort of halfway between a mountain bike and a road bike, the city bike is a great all-round choice for just plain riding. It comes with fat tires, which give you a softer ride, and upright handlebars. Unlike the handlebars of a mountain bike, the city bike's aren't straight. City bikes don't always have 18 gears, but they do come with good gear systems that make it easier to ride up hills and over longer distances. And city bikes are often lightweight enough to take some of the work out of getting around. In other words it's a comfortable bike.

Although you won't find kids' bikes sold in this category—or at least they aren't called city bikes in most stores—some of the better 20-inch kids' bikes have all the features of a city bike. With the features of a city bike, you get the ultimate in comfort, speed *and* climbing power.

MIDDLEWEIGHT BIKES OR CRUISERS

This is your basic bike, plain and simple. It has fenders, which a lot of other bikes don't have. (Fenders add weight.) It also comes with fat tires, a wider seat and upright handlebars. Some cruisers are three-speeds and some are single-speed bikes. They're fine for newspaper delivery routes, because they can take the extra weight and they tend to be very stable. But there's nothing fancy about a cruiser, and there aren't too many of them made these days. Cruisers are the bikes people choose if they don't want to shift gears or learn to ride with dropped handlebars. At the beach or in other areas that are flat, cruisers are sometimes available as rental bikes. In areas with hills, however, cruisers are not recommended because they're just too heavy and therefore difficult to pedal.

ROAD-RACING BIKES

To most people it looks just like any other adult road bike. But the road-racing bike is a mean machine in every sense of the word. Racing bikes

WHEEL FACTS

- As of 1988, touring bikes were the most popular style in America. However mountain bikes were increasing in popularity and moving up fast. More dollars were spent on mountain bikes than on any other style of bike in that same year.

are built with very light, stiff frames which help the athletes get top performance out of the bike. The stiff frame also makes for a very jarring, bumpy ride, however. You wouldn't want to ride a racing bike for pleasure, although to the athletes who compete in road races, these high-tech bicycles are a dream come true. The dream doesn't come cheaply. A good road-racing bike costs as much as $2,000 or more! Road-racing bikes are also used in triathlons—a racing event that combines swimming, biking and running.

TRACK-RACING BIKES

How would you like to jump on a bike with no brakes and no freewheel, which means that you couldn't coast? You probably wouldn't like it—unless you were competing at a track race. Track-racing bikes are built specifically for special indoor races and Olympic events.

These are very specialized bikes, so lightweight that they can't be ridden on regular pavement. If you want to keep moving forward, you have to keep pedaling every second! To slow down or stop, you have to pedal backwards. And their handling is so sensitive that it takes an expert rider to race them. You probably won't find track-racing bikes in your local neighborhood bike store. If you want to see one, head for the track—or the Olympics!

SPECIALIZED BIKES

If you've ever been to the circus, you've probably seen a *unicycle*. With only one wheel and no handlebars, how are you supposed to stay on those things? Practice, practice, practice! Kids as young as three years old have learned how to ride

a unicycle, and so could you. The secret is to get two people to help you—one on each side. (And get a book about unicycling too!)

Tandem bikes, on the other hand, seem like the opposite of unicycles. Tandem bikes have two seats, two sets of handlebars and two sets of pedals. With twice as much muscle power moving the bike, two people on a tandem can outrun one person on a high-speed racer easily!

Last but not least, how about a *folding bike*? Folding bikes are hinged in the middle of the frame, so that the front wheel can collapse on top of the back wheel. They are made for people who want to travel with their bikes, on boats or airplanes for instance. If you live in an apartment or have a *very* full garage, you might want a folding bike. Otherwise stick with one of the standard bikes. There are plenty to choose from!

ALL ABOUT BIKE SIZES

The very first thing you need to know when you buy a bike is whether or not the bike fits you. And that can change pretty quickly. Most kids outgrow their bikes about every two years! Still, it's *never* a good idea to buy a bike that you'll "grow into." Bikes are not sweaters. You can hurt yourself on a bike that's too big. Look for a bike that fits you now. Here's what you should know before you shop for a bike:

Bikes for kids are measured by the size of the wheel. Bikes for adults are measured by the size of the frame or, specifically, the length of the seat tube. Kids' bikes come in sizes ranging from 12- to 24-inch wheels. (That's the measurement of the diameter of, or the distance across, the wheel.) Adult bikes usually come in frame sizes ranging from 17 inches to 26 inches. If you are tall enough to straddle a bike with a 17-inch seat tube, you can buy an adult bike. For most kids, that happens at about age 14.

But how do you know if a bike is really the right size? Being able to climb on and reach the pedals isn't enough. You must be able to touch the ground, too! Otherwise you could fall off the seat and get hurt. *Never buy a bike that's too big for you.* If you are buying your first bike, remember:

You need to be able to balance on the seat, standing still, with your toes touching the ground.

WHAT ELSE TO LOOK FOR

In addition to size and style, you'll also want to consider the gear set that comes with a particular bike. This is especially important if you're buying an adult road bike, because not all 12-speed bikes are alike, and you'll want to get a bike that matches your own physical abilities. For now, just be aware that some bikes come with bigger, lower gears that help you climb hills more easily, while other bikes—the most expensive ones—don't have them. Why? Because people who are in top physical condition—professional and amateur athletes, for instance—don't want or need low

TRY IT!

Here are two tests you can do to see if a bike is the right size for you. Test Number 1: Straddle the bike but don't sit on the seat. Just stand over the top tube with both of your feet flat on the ground. There should be one or two inches between your crotch and the tube for a road bike. For a mountain bike, you'll need a gap of three inches. (Note: This test won't work on a girls' bike. To buy a woman's bike, use this test to get an accurate measurement on a standard bike frame. Then buy a woman's bike with the same-length seat tube.)

Test Number 2: Sit on the seat and have someone hold the handlebars so you won't fall over. Put your feet on the pedals and turn the crank until one pedal is straight down. (The other pedal will be straight up.) Have someone look at the leg that is extended down. It should be *almost* straight but not all the way. In other words, there should be a slight bend in your knee. If your knee is bent a lot, the seat needs to be raised—or the bike may be too small. You can raise the seat, but remember: *You must leave at least two inches of the stem inside the seat tube at all times!* After you've raised the seat, have someone check your leg extension. If your leg is more than slightly bent, it's time for a new bike.

If you're big enough to consider buying an adult-sized bike, you can get an idea about frame size by measuring your inseam or the inside of your leg. Stand flat on the floor in your biking shoes, and have someone measure the distance from your crotch to the floor. Then look at the chart below to find the frame size—or sizes—that are right for you.

Frame Size	Leg Length
17	26 to 30 inches
19	28 to 31 inches
20	29 to 32 inches
21	30 to 33 inches
22	31 to 34 inches
23	32 to 35 inches
24	33 to 36 inches
25	34 to 37 inches
26	35 to 38 inches

You'll notice that there is a lot of overlap in the frame sizes. A person with a 30-inch leg length, for instance, could choose a 17-inch, 19-inch, 20-inch or 21-inch frame. How you decide which size to buy will depend on the rest of your body and how it fits the rest of the bike.

Of course the best test for bike fit is to try it out and see if it's comfortable. If you feel that you are leaning too far forward or that you don't have control of the bike, don't buy it. Each bike design is different. With a little patience, you can easily find a bike that's right for you!

gears. You can read more about gears in Chapters 2 and 3.

Finally, when shopping for a new bike, you'll also want to ask about a bike's warranty. A warranty is a promise or guarantee from the bike manufacturer, and it usually covers any defects in workmanship or materials on the bike. In other words, if a chain rivet suddenly breaks off or the bike frame cracks under normal use, the bike company will replace the defective part free of charge. A one-year warranty on the frame is *not* considered to be a good warranty. That's like getting no warranty at all. You should expect a quality bike to have a lifetime warranty on the frame and a good company policy about repairs to parts. Ask also what the store's policy is. Some bike shops will give you an extended period of time in which to take advantage of the free tune-ups and adjustments that come with buying a new bike.

WHERE TO BUY A BIKE

If at all possible, buy your bike from a bike shop rather than from a toy store or discount store. Why? For a number of reasons. For one thing, the lower-priced bikes sold in huge discount stores are not built to last. The cheapest ones can fall apart the first time you fall off your bike. You may save a few dollars up front by buying a less expensive bike. But with a low-priced bike, you might have to replace the bike before you've actually outgrown it.

Your local bike shop is the place to go for bikes, parts, repairs and all-around good advice.

Another problem with discount-store bikes is that they are often put together by people who don't know much about bikes. When you buy a new bike, you want to know that the brakes are properly adjusted, the gears are all working smoothly, and the seat post has been tightened well—so you won't go flying off the first time you ride! In a good bike shop the employees know their stuff and will make sure that your bike is safe to ride *before* you take it out on the road. Many bike shops also offer additional services, such as a free bike tune-up within 30 days of purchase. And they will usually make adjustments without charge during the first 30 to 90 days after you buy the bike.

Does that mean you should never buy a bike from a discount store? No. Sometimes it pays to shop at them if they're selling reliable brand-name bikes. Or if you're buying a bike for the short term—in other words, if you expect to outgrow it pretty soon—then a less expensive bike can make sense. But try to avoid the least expensive bikes, especially the ones sold in discount stores. If your budget is tight, you're probably better off buying a good used bike. In any case be sure to check your new bike over carefully yourself. Don't count on the store employees to do it for you!

BUYING A USED BIKE

New bikes can be expensive, especially if you do outgrow your bike every two years. Buying a used bike can be a good way to save money and get a better quality bike than you might otherwise be able to afford. The trick is to find a good bike—one that was well made to start with and was taken care of by its previous owner. Here are some guidelines that will help you check out a used bike before you buy:

● The rule of thumb for buying a used bike is that *everything should operate smoothly*—that includes the wheels, the handlebars, the pedals and the chain. Make sure none of the moving parts grab or scrape when you move them.

● Look at the frame. If it is dented, rusted or cracked, forget it. If the bike frame was bent out of shape in an accident, it might not be safe or strong. If it's been repainted, make sure the new paint job isn't covering a crack. And, of course, make sure the frame fits you.

● Lift the bike up (or have a friend lift it for you) and spin the wheels. They should spin smoothly, with no wobble or side-to-side movement. The wheels should not touch or rub against any part of the bike when they are spinning. If the wheels aren't "true," don't buy the bike.

● Inspect the brake shoes or pads. If they are very worn, they will not be able to safely stop the bike. Badly worn brake pads are a clue that the bike has been ridden a lot. That's not bad—but it's a signal that you should look closely at each part of the bike. Other parts, such as the tires or brake cables, may be nearly as worn out as well. Then again, if worn brake pads are the *only* thing wrong with the bike, buy it—but make sure you change the brake pads right away!

● Squeeze the brake levers firmly. If the lever comes to within one inch of the handlebar, it means the brakes need to be adjusted.

● Check the tires to be sure there is some tread on them. Bald tires are dangerous.

● Grab the pedals in your hand and shake or twist them, trying to move the crank. The idea is to see whether there is any side-to-side movement, rattling or jiggling in the crank. There shouldn't be. The pedals should only move in a forward or backward circular motion.

● Make sure that every nut and bolt is properly tightened before riding the bike.

Whether you end up with a used three-speed or a brand new BMX, once you've gotten your bike you'll probably discover that it's easy to get psyched about any kind of cycling. Nothing beats the feeling of owning your own two wheels!

BIKE TALK

Bicyclists use their own slang to describe their sport. Here are a few of the phrases you might hear from veteran cyclists:

Bonking. Suddenly losing energy while riding a bicycle. It happens because all of your body's available carbohydrates have been used up.

Campy. Short for Campagnolo, the company that makes the very best parts (components) for bicycles. Campy invented the S.I.S. or synchro-index-shifting system, which makes shifting gears super-smooth. They also make forks, pedals and other parts. If you want to sound like you really know bikes, *never* say Campagnolo. Say Campy.

Granny Gears. Big freewheel gears which make hill climbing easier. Even though these gears have a wimpy name, lots of well-conditioned athletes use them. Only the toughest road warriors can do without granny gears on a steep hill.

Hit the Wall. This is something like bonking, but more severe. When you hit the wall, you've not only used up all of your body's fuel reserves, but you're burning up your own muscle tissue, too. Once you hit the wall, you're finished. Even stopping to eat won't give you enough of a boost to go on. This usually only happens to professionals racing over very long distances.

Honking. Nothing like bonking, this is what it's called when you hop off the seat, pedal standing up and really pull yourself up a hill.

Out the Window. Left behind the pack. Riders who are zooming ahead and leaving another rider behind say, "He's out the window."

Poseur. Someone who thinks he or she is a really swift biker, but isn't. A fake, in other words.

Road Rash. Scrapes from falling off your bike and getting skinned up.

Warriors. Very hard-working, tough cyclists. If someone calls you a warrior, it's a compliment. It means you can really battle it out on the road, and win.

IT'S A FRAME-UP!

Can you name the parts of your bike? And do you have any idea what each part is for? Or are you just out there flying on the wind, enjoying the sheer thrill of a high-speed ride down a smooth, open hill?

Flying on the wind is great—until something goes wrong. Then you'll need to work on your bike or have an expert fix it for you. At times like that it helps to know what all the parts are called and how they work. It also helps to understand a bicycle's body build—its anatomy—when you're shopping for a bike.

So here's the lowdown on how a bike is put together and how it functions like a mean machine, doing some of the work of moving you from place to place.

THE FRAME

This is the single most important element in a bicycle. The way the frame is designed, the materials used to make it, and the way it is put together all affect the way you feel when you ride. To a beginner, all bicycle frames might look alike—except for the color. But experienced cyclists know that there are dozens of differences in the basic diamond shape. (It might not look like a diamond to you, until you imagine the bike frame stripped down: no handlebars, no seat, no

gears, no wheels.) By changing the angles used to put that diamond frame together, bicycle designers can give you a comfortable ride—or a horribly stiff one. They can make it possible to jump over 3-foot hills on a BMX course or to reach speeds of 40 miles per hour on flat ground!

So when you're ready for an adult bike, remember that not all 20-inch frames are alike. The size of the bike frame determines whether or

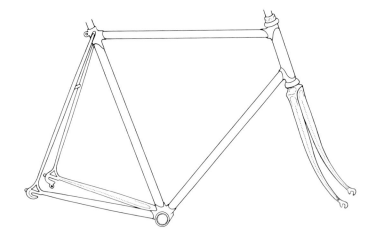

The classic diamond-shaped frame

not you can straddle it comfortably—but the angles used in the design determine how it feels, how it rides and whether or not you can reach the handlebars with ease. Stiff frames, with almost no "give" to them, are used by professional racers. The stiffer the frame, the more your energy is directed into forward movement. Flexible frames, on the other hand, take some of the shocks out of the ride. They absorb the bumps, making the bike more comfortable over long distances.

There's a lot of talk about frames and frame materials in the world of cycling. Most bikes are made of steel or a steel alloy (steel mixed with some other metals). But aluminum, titanium, magnesium and carbon fiber are also used for frames. Some bikes are made with tapered steel tubing to reduce the weight. With this type of tubing, the middle of the tube is thin but it becomes thicker near the joints where more strength is needed. Other bikes are lugged, which means that an extra collar of steel is wrapped around the tubing at each joint.

How do you know what to look for when you shop for a bike? On a kids' bike, you won't find the very best materials or welding techniques because you won't really need them. But you can look for quality. Check out the frame and use common sense. Does the frame look like it's well made? Is the paint evenly applied or is it cracked? Do the welded joints look strong, or do they look like they might come apart if you hit a pothole? Even if you have a limited budget, look at the more expensive bikes to get an idea of what a quality bike frame looks like. By comparing, you'll be more likely to notice the defects, if any, in the lower-priced bikes.

BIKE PARTS

The best way to learn the names of bike parts is to study the diagram on pages 14 to 15. It's all pretty logical: The top tube is on top, the down tube slants downward, the seat tube holds the stem of the seat, and the head tube is the short one at the very front or "head" of the bike. Those are the main, strongest structural parts of the frame. Then there are the chain stays, which run more or less parallel to the chain, and the seat stays, which slant down from the seat to the rear hub. Last but definitely not least is the fork. You can't miss the fork—it splits open like the tines of a fork at the front of the bike, holding the front wheel to the head tube. You don't really need to memorize

these terms, but it's helpful to know them if you ever want to work on your bike.

Other important parts of your bike are the bottom bracket, chain, crank, derailleur (de-RAIL-er) and brakes.

In the next section, you'll find out all about the brains and brawn of your bicycle—the derailleur gear system.

HOW GEAR COMBINATIONS WORK

Very simply, gears help you do some of the work of pedaling your bike. They help the wheels spin. Low gears help you pedal uphill easily, middle gears are used on flat ground, and high gears help you to go super fast—although high gears are harder to pedal than the others are.

Here's how gear combinations work together:

● When the gear near the crank (the chainwheel) is larger than the gear in back (the freewheel), it takes more energy to pedal—but you go farther forward.

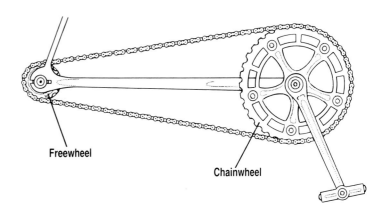

Chain wheel, chain, and free wheel on a fixed-gear bike

● When the gear near the crank is smaller than the freewheel gear, it's easier to pedal—but you don't go as far.

What this means is that when your bike is in a low gear, you can turn the pedals one time around with your legs and go forward several feet. But in a high gear, one revolution of the pedals will take you twice as far!

If you want to understand how gears work, forget about bikes for a minute.

Have you ever seen an egg beater? If you have

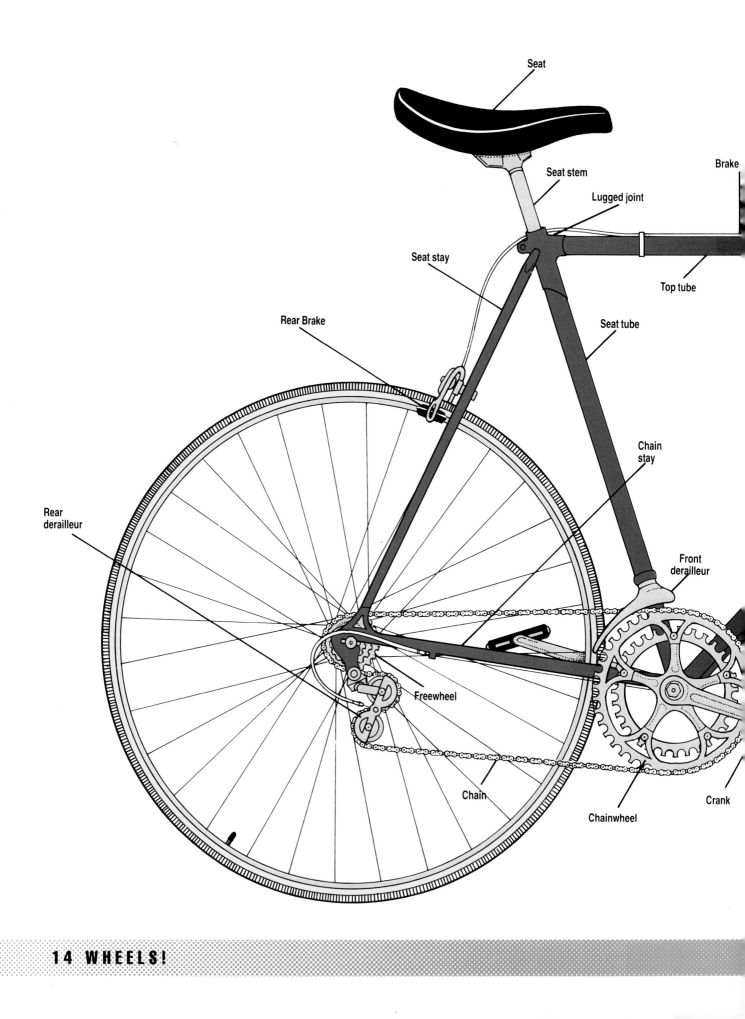

Seat

Brake

Seat stem

Lugged joint

Top tube

Seat stay

Seat tube

Rear Brake

Chain
stay

Rear
derailleur

Front
derailleur

Freewheel

Chain

Crank

Chainwheel

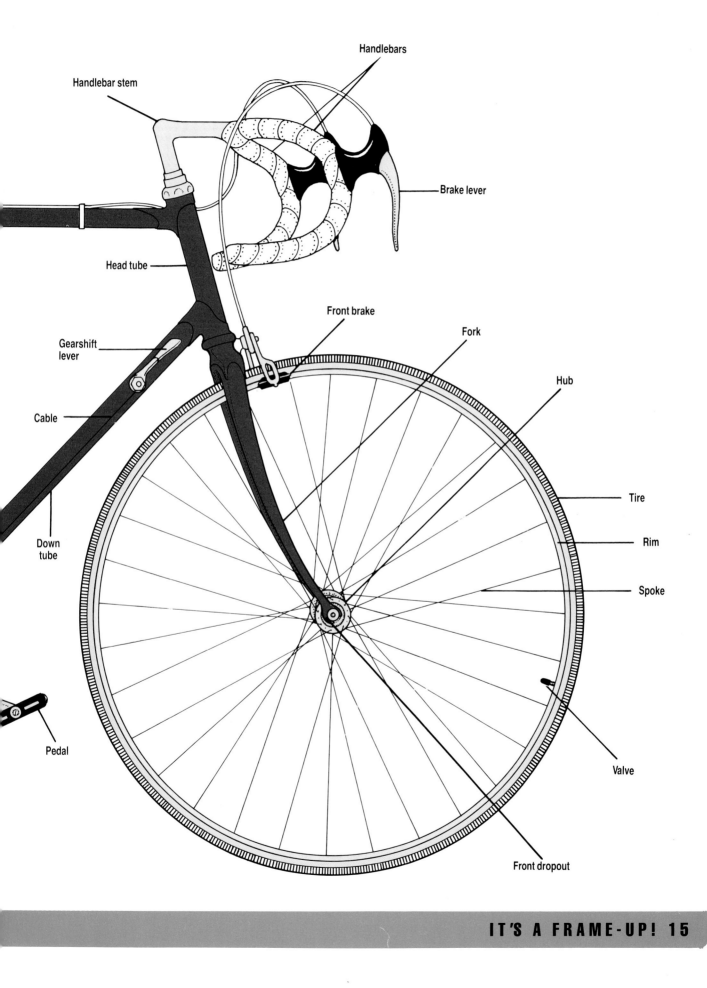

Handlebars

Handlebar stem

Brake lever

Head tube

Front brake

Fork

Hub

Gearshift lever

Cable

Tire

Rim

Spoke

Down tube

Pedal

Valve

Front dropout

one, take a look at it. It's a simple machine, consisting of a crank, three gears and two beaters. Each part of the machine does a different job. The beaters, of course, mix up the eggs or food. The gears make the beaters go around. And the crank makes the gears go around.

Imagine what it would be like trying to use an egg beater with either the crank or the gears missing. Could you just hold the two beaters in your hands and twirl them? No. You couldn't spin them fast enough or with enough force to mix the food. Could you do without the crank? Could you turn the top gear with your fingers alone? No way. It would be too much work. The crank and the gears each do some of the work for you.

Believe it or not, a bike is a lot like an egg beater. You've got a crank—that's what the pedals are attached to. And just as on an egg beater, the crank turns one gear which turns another. In this case the pedals turn the front gear, called the *chainwheel*. The chainwheel turns the back gear, called the *freewheel*. The bike is different from the egg beater in that the gears don't actually touch each other. They are separated by some empty space—but they're connected by the chain. The chain transfers the energy from one gear to the other. And when the back gear turns, it turns the back wheel of the bike. (The front wheel, as you may have noticed, isn't part of the gear system. It's just there for balance. It gets pushed along in front of everything else.)

But wait a minute, you say. Egg beaters are really nothing like 12-speed bikes, are they? I mean, you can't shift gears on an egg beater, can you?

Right. An egg beater is nothing like a 12-speed bike. An egg beater is like a *single-speed* bike! The point is that *even if you only have a single-speed bike,* you are getting the benefits of a gear system which helps you do some of the work. A multispeed bike, on the other hand, uses gears of different sizes to do different kinds of work.

WHAT'S A DERAILLEUR?

In the world of multispeed biking, things didn't really start to move until the derailleur was invented. Derailleur is a French word which means to "derail" the chain, or push it off the rail or track. (There is no actual rail on a bicycle. The derailleur pushes the chain from one cog or gear to the next.) When you press a gear shift lever on a derailleur-equipped bike, the lever moves a cable which moves the derailleur. Since the chain is riding on the derailleur, the chain is forced to move, too. It moves from one size sprocket, or gear, to another.

Some bikes come with 5-speed derailleurs. But most derailleur systems are 12-speeds or more. With a 12-speed bike you'll have 2 gears or sprockets in front and 6 in back, for a total of 12 combinations. On a 15-speed bike you'll have 3 sprockets in front and 5 in back. Then there's the 18-speed bike, with 3 in front and 6 in back. For all of these bikes you'll need two derailleurs and two gear shift levers to control them. Don't worry, though—you don't always have to shift both derailleurs at the same time. Many times you'll just want to shift up to the next higher gear, which can mean shifting only the rear set of sprockets. On the other hand, there are times when you'll want to go from first gear to tenth, skipping all the others in between.

There is one time, though, when you shouldn't do this. If you are riding on flat ground in a high gear, and suddenly you come to a hill, *don't* shift

TRY IT!

If you're still not sure how gears help you do the work, try this. Find a record player with a regular turntable. Try to spin the turntable by holding only the little spindle in the center with your thumb and forefinger. It's hard work! But you can easily spin the turntable from the outer edge. All you have to do is give it a one-fingered push. Having small gears on a bike is like trying to spin the turntable from the center spindle. It just takes more work. When you have larger gears, it's like transferring the work closer to the outside edge of the turntable—or the wheel, in this case.

WHEEL FACTS

- **Bicycling burns about 300 to 500 calories per hour, depending on how fast you go. This is a measure of how hard your body works when you ride. Compare it to playing basketball, which burns 327 calories an hour, baseball which burns 218, swimming (the crawl) which burns 227, and sitting still, which burns about 60 calories per hour.**

from your highest gear to your lowest hill-climbing gear all at once. When the bike and the derailleur are under pressure—the pressure you exert when you're starting up a hill—the parts can't take a sudden and extreme shift. The derailleur could break in two. So be sure to shift gradually when coming to a hill.

One last important note: Never lay a bike down on its right side—on top of the derailleur, in other words. The derailleur is a delicate part, and you can damage it that way.

FUTURE GEARS

In recent years many great new ways to shift gears have been developed. Click shifting is one of the latest improvements, and by the time you read this, some kids' bikes will have click shifting. Very simply, click shifting makes it easier for you to find a certain gear because the gear shift lever actually clicks into place at each position. Without click shifting, you have to guess-timate the correct position for each gear, and sometimes you miss. When that happens you hear a grinding or rattling noise which means that you haven't quite slipped the chain into the right place. Then you have to push the gear shift lever a little bit farther forward or back.

A new trend for mountain bikes is a thumb shifter located *under* the handlebars. It's easier to reach there, without moving your hands from their do-or-die competitive grip!

And how about aerobars? These are the handlebars that road racers started using in the late 1980s. Aerobars sweep forward, providing small padded spots for the racer's arms to rest on. In that position, the racer can't easily reach down to a gear shift lever on the bicycle frame—which is where the shifter is usually located on a racing bike. So these bikes come equipped with bar-end shifters. All you do is twist the end of the aerobar. It's just like unscrewing a bottle cap!

BRAKES

There are basically two kinds of brakes: coaster brakes and caliper brakes. Coaster brakes are activated by pedaling backwards. They are very safe and effective because they are located inside the hub of the rear wheel, so they always stay dry. Since there are no cables involved with coaster brakes, they never break down or go out of adjustment. So why would anyone want anything else?

The problem with coaster brakes is that you can't get going quickly from a dead stop. Since you have to pedal backwards to engage the brakes, you also have to pedal forwards to disengage the brakes. In other words, there is a "loose" spot in the pedaling action. In a race, or even in everyday riding, you lose time trying to get going again. You have to pedal forward half a revolution before the gears even begin to move the bicycle forward.

Caliper brakes consist of two brake "shoes" or pads. The shoes are attached to a U-shaped clamp. These brakes work by gripping the rim of the tire and slowing it down. When you squeeze the brake

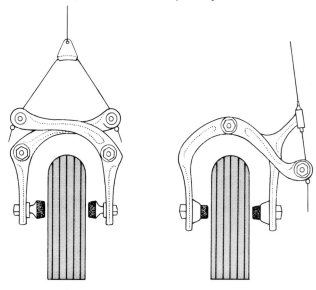

lever on the handlebars, it pulls on the brake cable, making it shorter. The more you pull on the brake cable, the harder the brake shoes grip the rim of the wheel. There are three main kinds of caliper brakes: side-pull, center-pull and cantilever brakes. They are all pictured on this page and the previous page.

You can read more about adjusting your brakes in Chapter 6. But here is a very important safety tip to remember: If you have center-pull caliper brakes and you raise or lower your handlebars, *you must readjust your brakes*. Why? Because you will have changed the length of the brake cable, making the brakes too loose or too tight. Either way, they won't work! Unless you have a lot of experience with bike repairs, take your bike to a bike shop and let the pros make this adjustment for you.

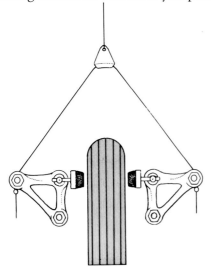

TRY IT!

If you have a multispeed bike, here's an experiment you can do to prove to yourself how your bicycle's gears work. Grab a piece of chalk and take it to a sidewalk or empty parking lot. Ride your bike, shifting gears, until you are in your lowest gear—the largest freewheel sprocket. Now hop off your bike and draw a chalk line on the sidewalk. Position your front tire on the chalk line and position the pedals so that the right pedal is straight up at the 12 o'clock position. Roll your bike *backwards* in a straight line until the pedals have gone around once. The right pedal will be back at 12 o'clock again. Draw a chalk line where your front tire is now. The distance between the two chalk lines is the distance that you can travel with one revolution of your pedals in low gear.

Now climb on your bike and get it into your highest gear. Position your bike on the front chalk line and repeat the experiment, rolling your bike backwards for one full revolution of the pedals. You'll be amazed to see how much farther you can go! We tried it on a 5-speed kids' bike with 20-inch wheels. One revolution in the lowest gear took the bike 6 feet, 10 inches. The highest gear took the bike almost 15 feet!

Why does this experiment have to be done in reverse? Because multispeed bikes with derailleur gear systems have something called a freewheel in back. The freewheel allows you to coast forward even if you aren't pedaling. If you rolled your bike forward, some of the distance you traveled could be "coasting" distance, not distance covered by pedaling. Try walking your bike forward, and you'll see that the pedals don't go around. The freewheel doesn't work the same way in reverse, though.

CYCLE SEARCH

The first bicycles were strange-looking machines with even stranger names. Some of the names given to bicycles of the 1800s are hidden in the word search below. The words may be written in any direction—even upside down and backward! Can you find all *eight* of them?

Boneshaker   Hobbyhorse   Safety

Facile   Penny Farthing   Velocipede

High-wheeler   Ordinary

```
H I P R C L A P D F E Y
E D E P I C O L E V A L
B O N E S H A K E R S C
G E N P R A I K G A F T
U R Y E R M S I F O A O
T R F E L C I E H B C R
E N A Q U A T O O R I D
E S R O H Y B B O H L I
D A T V M E P H I N E N
A B H A F S O I G B P A
S H I G H W H E E L E R
N O N T R E I S P L A Y
I L G O U C R A Y M V E
```

Answers on p. 79.

CHAPTER 3

RIDING! TIPS & TECHNIQUES

Even if you've been riding for years, chances are you might not know all the techniques that can turn you into a real cyclist. What about shifting gears? And what about hand brakes? If your first bike didn't have those features, you may never have learned how to use them. There's a lot to learn—everything from how to shift gears to how to stop on a gravel-covered hill, and a whole lot in between. So before you start your pedals, take some time to read about the techniques you can put into action. Even if you think you're a pro, read on. There are special tips for advanced riders.

DON'T READ THE REST OF THIS CHAPTER YET

Not until you promise to follow rule Number 1. What's rule Number 1? It's the rule that can save your life: *Always wear a helmet!* No matter how much of a hotshot you are on your bike, the street is a dangerous place. Come on—there are cars out there! And crazy drivers too. Besides, it's not cool to crack your skull on the pavement. So if you don't have a helmet, get one. Take a tip from the pros and wear one every time you go out.

GIVE ME A BRAKE!

Check out your bike. If it has hand-operated brakes, you'll see that one control operates the front brake and one operates the rear brake. Should you use them both at the same time—or one and then the other? The answer depends on the situation.

For regular riding on fairly flat, smooth pavement in dry weather, use this technique. Apply your rear brake first, and then just a second or two later apply your front brake. Both brakes work the same way, and they apply the same amount of force to stop the wheels. But the results are different. The front brake tends to stop the whole front end of the bike—instantly! When the bike stops too suddenly, your body tends to keep going because you have momentum. By applying the back brake just a little bit before the front one, you slow your momentum. Then when you apply the front brake you won't go flying over the handlebars. That's called doing an "endo" (because your body goes end over end) and it's definitely to be avoided!

Attention: Left-handed Riders! On most bikes, the left-handed brake lever controls the front brake. So you have to be particularly careful

WHEEL FACTS

- **Many professional athletes, including tennis star Ivan Lendl, use bicycling to help them get in shape for their own sport. John McEnroe and boxer Sugar Ray Leonard have also been known to work out on two wheels.**

about that lever. Your left hand may be stronger, or you may have a tendency to squeeze it first instead of second. It's something to be aware of.

However, don't think that just because the front brake is so powerful, you shouldn't use it. In fact, you *need* to use it. Because of the science and physics involved, your front brake is responsible for doing most of the work in stopping your bike.

When you get a new bike, it's a good idea to practice braking until you really know your bike and know what it can do. Different conditions mean you have to use different brake techniques.

For instance, in wet weather your brakes won't work as well. You'll have to apply them sooner and allow more time to stop. Try to apply both brakes at the same time, but squeeze gently at first. Then release and squeeze again. You don't want to skid on the wet pavement, and this slow braking technique will give you time to judge how well your brakes are working. Don't forget that "wet weather" can mean a perfectly sunny day if you've just ridden through a huge puddle or a stream. The water on your tires and brakes reduces the braking action.

On a downhill, put on the brakes long before you want to stop. If it's a steep hill, you'll probably want to use the brakes on and off lightly all the way down the hill. Don't coast down hills at top speed—even if the coast seems to be clear. You never know when someone is going to pull out from a driveway or turn into the street you're riding on.

For gravel-covered surfaces, and especially if you're coming down a gravel or loose-surfaced hill, be sure to apply the brakes gradually. Use the on-and-off technique here too. That way you'll find out just how slippery the dirt or gravel is.

Should you ever grab both brakes at once and squeeze hard? Yes—in an emergency. If you need to stop instantly, to avoid being hit by a car for instance, you'll have to use the full power of both brakes. Still, you should try to apply the brakes gradually—*fast* but gradually. It's tricky! Hold on tight, and try to lean back or shift your weight toward the back of your bike. That will help to counterbalance the effects of the super-fast stop.

COASTER BRAKES

With coaster brakes, the harder you pedal backwards, the quicker you'll stop. There are no special rules for using coaster brakes—just follow the same guidelines as for hand brakes:

- Always use your brakes when coming down a hill.
- Apply your brakes gradually on a gravel-covered surface.
- Remember to brake carefully in wet weather, so that you won't skid on wet pavement.

Coaster brakes have one advantage over hand brakes—they don't get wet when it rains because they are located *inside* the rear hub. (The hub is the cylinder that holds the axle of the wheel.)

SHIFTING GEARS FOR BEGINNERS

This section is only for people who have derailleur gear systems. Some 3-speed bikes have derailleurs, but most do not. If you've got a simple 3-speed bike with the gear shifting mechanism located inside the rear axle, skip ahead to "Shifting the 3-Speed."

Now, for the rest of you biking maniacs out there, hold on to your helmets. The whole subject of gears can get a little complicated—especially if you have more than 10-speeds.

As a beginner, the first thing you need to know is *you must be pedaling when you shift gears*. If you're not, you can damage your derailleur system. The second thing you should know is that you don't really *have* to shift gears at all if you don't want to. Gears are there to help you get up hills more easily and to take some of the work out of biking. If you don't shift, you won't hurt your bike—you'll just tire yourself out sooner. So if you've just gotten a new bike and you aren't sure when to shift, don't worry about it. You'll figure it out eventually. In the meantime just have fun.

Here's the simplest way to remember which gears are used for which situations:

Low gears are the larger gears on the rear or freewheel combined with the smallest gear on the front or chainwheel. If you want to use numbers for your gears, give these gears the lower numbers. Low gears take a low amount of effort, so they are used for climbing hills.

Middle gears take a medium amount of effort. They are used on flat ground. You'll probably use your middle gears more than anything else.

High gears take a high amount of effort because the gears aren't doing as much of the work for you. You are in your highest gear when the chain is on the smallest freewheel gear (in back) and the largest chainwheel gear (in front). High gears are used for riding downhill and/or for going fast.

Understanding gears gets very tricky if you have more than one size gear on the chainwheel. Why? Because if you want to shift gears in order, from lowest to highest, you can't just push the gear shift levers forward one notch at a time. The exact gear you're in depends on the *combination*—which front gear combined with which rear gear.

There are two gear combinations that you should try to avoid. Don't ride with the largest chainwheel gear combined with the largest freewheel gear. And don't use the smallest with the smallest either. These two combinations tend to wear out your chain faster.

More than this you don't need to know until you've gotten used to your bike. In the meantime let your riding experiences tell you which gears to use.

SHIFTING GEARS FOR ADVANCED RIDERS

Let's say you just bought a new 15-speed bike. You want to know which gear combinations will be low, middle and high gears. What you need to do is figure out the gear ratio and the gear "inches" for each combination.

Gear ratio and gear inches are numbers that you can find one of two ways: by doing some mathematical formulas or by looking at a chart on which the math has already been done for you.

(There's a chart on page 23.) Whichever method you use, when you find the answer, you and all the other cyclists in the world will be able to talk to each other about cycling! Everyone in cycling knows, for instance, that a 30-inch gear combination is a low gear. Low gears range from 20 gear inches to about 40 gear inches. Middle gears, for cruising around, usually fall into the 40 to 65 gear-inch range. High gears are usually in the 70s, 80s and 90s.

But 90 *what*, you might ask. Why is it called 90 inches and what do these numbers mean? It's a good question—especially since you probably can't find *anything* on your bike that's 90 inches long.

The truth is, the term "gear inches" is left over from the early days of bicycling. The number refers to the size of wheel you would need to have in front if you were riding a *single*-speed, old-fashioned bike. But you're not—and that's not the important point, anyway. What's important is that once you know which gears are which—low, middle and high—you'll be able to make the best use of your bike.

The formula to find the gear inches for your bike is simple: You just divide the number of teeth in the front sprocket, or chainwheel, by the number of teeth in the rear sprocket, or freewheel, and then multiply by the diameter of your rear wheel. (The diameter is the distance across the middle of a circle.) Here's how the formula is written:

$$\text{Gear inches} = \frac{\text{teeth in front sprocket}}{\text{teeth in rear sprocket}} \times \frac{\text{diameter}}{\text{of real wheel}}$$

So the first thing you need to know is how big your rear wheel is. If you're not sure, measure the diameter—from one outside edge of the tire, straight across the middle hub to the opposite outside edge. Then you need to know how many teeth there are on each sprocket on your bike. You might have to count them, but first look on the sprocket itself. The number of teeth is often stamped into the metal.

If your bike has a rear wheel diameter to match the one in this chart, you can use it to find the gear inches for each gear combination. If your bike is smaller, get out the calculator and good luck!

GEAR RATIO CHART FOR BIKE WITH 27″ WHEELS
(rounded to the nearest whole number)

NUMBER OF TEETH IN CHAINWHEEL (FRONT GEAR)

NUMBER OF TEETH IN FREEWHEEL (REAR GEAR)

	24	26	28	30	32	34	36	38	40	42	44	46	48	50	52
12	54	58	63	68	72	77	81	86	90	95	99	104	108	113	117
14	46	50	54	58	62	66	69	73	77	81	85	89	93	96	100
15	43	47	50	54	58	61	65	68	72	76	79	83	86	90	94
16	41	44	47	51	54	57	61	64	68	71	74	78	81	84	88
17	38	41	44	48	51	54	57	60	64	67	70	73	76	79	83
18	36	39	42	45	48	51	54	57	60	63	66	69	72	75	78
19	34	37	40	43	45	48	51	54	57	60	63	65	68	71	74
20	32	35	38	41	43	46	49	51	54	57	59	62	65	68	70
21	31	33	36	39	41	44	46	49	51	54	57	59	62	64	67
22	29	32	34	37	39	42	44	47	49	52	54	56	59	61	64
23	28	31	33	35	38	40	42	45	47	49	52	54	56	59	61
24	27	29	32	34	36	38	41	43	45	47	50	52	54	56	59
25	26	28	30	32	35	37	39	41	43	45	48	50	52	54	56
26	25	27	29	31	33	35	37	39	42	44	46	48	50	52	54
27	24	26	28	30	32	34	36	38	40	42	44	46	48	50	52
28	23	25	27	29	31	33	35	37	39	41	42	44	46	48	50
29	22	24	26	28	30	32	34	35	37	39	41	43	45	47	48
30	22	23	25	27	29	31	32	34	36	38	40	41	43	45	47

If your chainwheel has an odd number of teeth, or if you can't find your gears on this chart, you still get the gear ratio using the formula on page 22.

SHIFTING THE 3-SPEED

Unlike a derailleur gear system, the gear system of a basic 3-speed is not shifted while pedaling. In fact, it's the opposite. You need to stop pedaling for a moment, shift and then start pedaling again. First gear is the low gear, easiest to pedal. It helps you get up hills. Second gear is the middle gear, for average flat-surface riding. Third gear is a high gear used to build up speed.

PEDALING

Hey—it's simple. You just hop on your bike and ride, right? Right. Some people may tell you that you need to learn a fancy technique called ankling. And it's true—ankling is the best way to pedal. But the truth of the matter is that just about everyone "ankles" automatically. It's kind of the natural way to pedal, just as putting one foot in front of the other is the natural way to walk.

As long as you're pedaling with the ball of your foot on the pedal—and you should be—you're probably already ankling. To ankle, you simply point your toes downward *slightly* on the downstroke, and let them point up *slightly* at the top of the stroke. One advantage to ankling is that it helps you get your foot into position to *push* through the stroke, even before your foot is at the top. But don't worry about ankling—it comes naturally. Do worry, however, if you're in the bad habit of pedaling with your weight on the middle of your foot, at the arch. That's where all the nerves in your foot are located, and you can do serious damage that way.

CORNERING

The only trick to cornering is to keep your inside leg and pedal raised to the top as you make the turn. Your inside leg is the leg that's inside the curve you're making. Another way to say that is: If you're turning right, your right leg is inside. If you're turning left, your left leg is inside. With your inside pedal raised, your weight is distributed to avoid a fall. If your inside leg and pedal are down, you can easily slide out and crash.

GET A GRIP

Hand position. Is there a trick to it?

Yes, if you have dropped handlebars. No, if you have straight bars.

For dropped handlebars, you'll probably want to change your hand position from time and time. That's the best way to avoid putting too much pressure on any one part of your hand. There are four positions that work with dropped bars. They are:

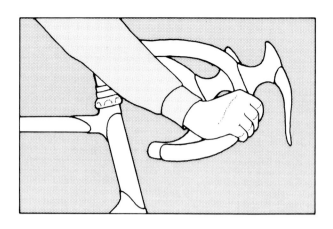

- Hands on the very ends of the grips—good for climbing hills. Pull up on the bar as you pedal.

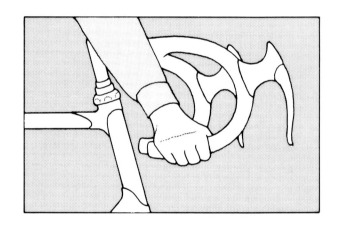

- Hands near the top of the bars, palms up with thumbs on top. This is a good variation because it helps you distribute your weight to a different part of your hand.

- Hands on top of the bars, close to the handlebar stem, knuckles facing up. This position is good for sightseeing because you are more upright.

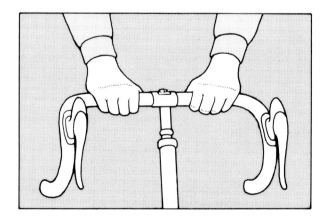

- Hands in the curve, just under the brake levers. Use this position when riding in traffic or downhill, so that you'll be able to reach the brakes easily.

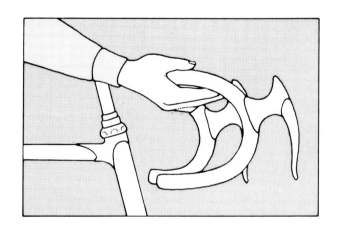

PLAY IT SAFE

No matter how radical you are on your bike, you can't always outmaneuver the other people on the road—namely motorists. So you've got to play it safe, and that means following all the rules of the road. Here they are, short and sweet. Read them and then follow them, because biking accidents are no joke. Who do you think is going to lose in a contest between a 2,000-pound four-wheeler and a 100-pound two-wheeler?

• Always wear a helmet. Even in your own driveway you can land on your head!

• Obey all traffic rules, beginning with the most obvious one: Always ride on the right side of the road, *with* the traffic.

• Wait your turn at intersections. Don't sneak up on cars that are stopped at traffic lights by riding up beside them. Bikers are notorious for doing this. You might think that it's okay, since there's plenty of room between the car and curb—but forget it! So many things can go wrong. The motorist might suddenly decide to turn right, even while the light is red. (Many states allow right turns on red.) Or someone might suddenly hop out of the passenger side, hitting you with the door. Stay behind the motor traffic, and wait the extra few seconds for *your* turn to go through the intersection.

• Always turn from the proper lane. This means that you only turn right from the right lane, and only turn left from the left lane. No exceptions!

• Always signal your turns using hand signals. The standard hand signals are done using your left arm. To turn left, stick your arm straight out. To turn right, extend your arm and bend your elbow so your hand goes up—almost like you are waving to someone. To signal a stop, hold your left arm out and down at an angle, with your palm spread wide open.

• Never weave in and out of traffic.

• Ride cautiously when passing parked cars. Many accidents occur when a motorist or passenger suddenly opens a car door into the path of an approaching cyclist.

• Watch for pedestrians and give them the right-of-way.

• Don't ride at night—it's too dangerous.

• If you *mus*[...]
This is the most re[...]
can see most easily at n[...]
jacket or sweatshirt that ha[...]
You can buy the tape in most b[...]
on yourself and on your bike, or ad[...]
reflectors such as the micro-prism reflec[...]
mentioned on page 33. *Night riding is very [...]
dangerous and should be avoided.* If you get caught away from home after dark, consider walking your bike home, calling someone to come get you or, at the very least, riding on the sidewalk.

• If you ride on a cloudy day, you might want to wear neon pink; it's more noticeable than any other color in daylight.

• Be extra careful when entering the street from your driveway or a sidewalk. Motorists aren't expecting you. Start slowly.

• Forget about the idea of using a whistle or bell to "warn" other motorists of your approach. Whistles are just a careless cyclist's way of saying "Here I come, so you'd better look out!" If you're following all the traffic rules, motorists won't have to "look out" for you. You'll be looking out for yourself.

• Check your bike—especially the brakes—to be sure everything is working properly each time you go out.

• If you ride on sidewalks, be very careful around pedestrians. Always pass them on the left. Some towns and cities don't allow cycling on sidewalks, so find out what the laws are in your area.

• Be a careful rider and help to change the statistics. About half of all serious bicycle accidents happen to children age 16 or younger. Boys from age 10 to 16 have more bike accidents than any other age group. Don't let it happen to you!

t ride at night, always wear
ective color, the one white.
ght. Better yet, wear a
s reflective tape on it,
king stores. Put it
d some extra
rors

Freestyle at its finest!

TRIVIA MATCH

Complete each piece of trivia on the left with the correct number from the colum[n] answers on the right.

1. Cycling champion Greg LeMond usually rides about this many races in the spring to get ready for the Tour de France.

2. A cyclist going down a mountain road can go this many miles per hour.

3. Some people can ride unicycles that are this many feet tall.

4. What is the most number of people who ever sat on a standard bicycle at one time, according to the *Guinness Book of World Records?*

5. Sean O'Keefe was this many years old when he rode almost 3,000 miles across the United States on a bicycle.

A) 11
B) 80
C) 60
D) 16
E) 100

Answers on page 79.

CHAPTER 4

GET INTO GEAR!

Half the fun of owning a bike is all the cool accessories you can buy to go with it. Biking gear, we call it. Some of these things are necessities—equipment you need in order to be safe. Some of the gear is used to carry other gear. And some of these extras are just plain fun! Here's a rundown, starting with the stuff you really need.

HELMETS

Don't leave home without them! You're going to hear about helmets at least twice more before you finish reading this book. That's because helmets are real lifesavers. Broken bones will mend and scraped knees will heal. But head injuries can last a lifetime—or *end* a life. You can't bang up your head the way you can the rest of your body. Your brain just can't take it.

The best helmets are the ones that give you a lot of padding and protection. So forget about the skimpy helmets with padded tubes of black leather crisscrossing your head. They are too open, too soft and they leave too much of your head exposed. The best biking helmets are made of Styrofoam with a cloth or plastic covering. They have vents so you won't sweat, and extra pads you can put inside to make the helmet fit just right. Some companies make helmets just for kids. If you can't find a kid-sized helmet to fit you, ask

for an adult size extra-small. It may work just as well.

Most people wait until they've been in a serious accident before buying a helmet. That's a lot like waiting until your bike has been stolen to get a good lock.

LOCKS

Unfortunately, locks are a necessity. Bikes are easy to steal and thousands of them are stolen every year. Parts are stolen from locked bikes, and even locked bikes are stolen by thieves who carry chain cutters! If you live in a medium-sized or large city, you shouldn't think twice about what kind of lock to buy. The U-shaped heavy metal locks are absolutely the best—particularly with an adult bike. The only drawback to using a U-shaped lock is that it doesn't enclose both front and back wheels at the same time—unless you remove the front wheel and lock it side by side with the back. Always put the lock around the wheel *and* the frame. Watch out for cheap imitations of these locks. Some of the fakes can easily be cut with bolt-cutters or hacksaws.

Many people prefer to use plastic-covered chains and cables because they are lighter in weight. These are not as secure as U-shaped locks, but you'll have to decide what's best for your hometown area after checking with neighbors and friends. Remember that *all* chains and cables can be cut with the tools that thieves use. If you use a chain, it should be at least one-quarter inch thick and six-feet long. The lock should be a heavy-duty padlock with a key, not a combination lock. Combination locks are easy to smash and break. Be sure to loop the chain or cable through both wheels and around the frame as well as wrap it around something that can't be moved: a parking meter, a tree, a railing or a signpost. And be sure that your bike can't be lifted up *over* the parking meter—chain and all! If you don't lock up both wheels, you might come back and find them missing. Professional thieves will steal anything—a whole bike or whatever parts are available.

In addition to a lock, you should protect your bike by registering it with the police. In many communities the police will come to your house and engrave an ID number on your bike—or they'll let you use their engraving tool, free of charge. They'll also give you an Operation ID decal to put on your bike. If your bike is stolen, you'll have to prove that you own it in order to get it back. The ID number helps, especially if you've lost your sales receipt or forgotten your bike's serial number.

Here are some more tips for protecting your bike:

● Be especially careful at shopping centers, playgrounds, bike shops and bicycle races or group events. Bike thieves like to hang around these spots because there are usually so many bikes there. The thief won't be noticed in the crowd if he or she hops on your bike and rides off.

● When your bike is mounted on a bike rack on a car, lock it to the rack. That way, the bike is protected when your family leaves the car during a trip.

● If you ride to school everyday, you could leave your lock at school. Lock it to the bicycle rack, and it will be waiting for you when you get there each day.

● Remember that your bike accessories can be stolen even if your bike is locked.

TIRE PUMPS AND GAUGES

You'll need a tire pump no matter what, even if you own a whole chain of gas stations! Bicycle tires need to be inflated carefully so they don't explode. Gas station air pumps are too powerful and too difficult to control. Buy a lightweight tubular pump and an air-pressure gauge. The gauge measures how many pounds of air pressure you have put into your tire. You need it so you can make sure the tire is inflated properly. You can also get a clamp, so that the pump can be attached to the bike frame. For long-distance trips or bicycle touring, you'll want the clamp so you can take the pump along. But for short local rides, leave your pump at home. The chances are greater that the pump will be stolen than that you'll have a flat tire!

WATER BOTTLES

This is one of the coolest accessories around—in every sense of the word! Drinking water keeps you cool during a long, hot summer ride. In fact, the experts recommend that you take a few slurps every 20 to 30 minutes. In hot weather your body may need as much as a full bottle of water every hour. Water bottles look cool, too. They come in every color imaginable. You can even get a bottle to match the color of your bike. The bottle rides in a cage that is bolted or clamped to the down tube on your bike, so you can reach it while cycling. Ask a bike-shop clerk to help you mount the cage on your bike.

BIKING CLOTHES

Let's face it. Biking shorts look great. They tell the world that you're really into biking, you're cool, and you're a radical human being! (Radical as a slang word was originally a biking term, by the way. It comes from California, where kids first did truly "radical" stunts on their BMX freestyle bikes.) Racing shorts also serve a purpose. They cut down on wind resistance and keep your legs free to pedal. And since there's a seamless piece of soft cloth in the crotch—called a chamois—they also eliminate chafing and rubbing on a long ride. Last but not least, biking clothes are made of a special material that absorbs perspiration and then allows it to evaporate quickly, so you stay cool and dry.

Biking shirts, called jerseys, will also keep you cool and dry, and like the shorts, they fit tightly to cut down on wind resistance. Often they've got

Dressed to race, a BMX rider in full gear: helmet, face and chest protectors, gloves and "leathers."

WHEEL FACTS

- **Everyone seems to want to ride their bikes in the snow. Mountain bike fanatics in Northern California have started snow cycling for a really cool thrill. They hold downhill competitions, like skiers. And in Alaska, there's a race called the Iditabike which follows part of the same frozen course used by dogsledders in the famous Iditarod.**

three pockets on the back—for directions, change or even a quick snack.

If you race BMX or do freestyle stunts, you'll want the special long-sleeved, long-legged, padded BMX "leathers" that not only protect you but also give you a look that's *really* radical!

SHOES

Serious bikers and racers wear bicycle shoes with cleats on the bottom. The cleats help keep the cyclist's foot on the pedals. If you're ready for cleated shoes, you're also ready for a more advanced book about cycling. (See the Appendix for suggested reading.)

Most people, however, just need a pair of ordinary high-top athletic shoes. High-tops are important because they protect you against the effects of a certain kind of accident that has happened all too often. When you fall off your bike in just the wrong way, your foot can get jammed between the ground and the pedal. With enough pressure, the pedal can cut into your heel and do a *lot* of damage. "I saw my bone," one 10-year-old girl said recently, after a biking accident which required 30 stitches in her heel. "It was gross." If you don't want to be grossed out by your own anatomy, wear high-top sneakers for biking safety.

TOE CLIPS

Toe clips are small metal bands which attach to the bicycle pedal. Together with a strap that can

be loosened and tightened like a belt, toe clips work to keep your foot on the pedal. They also increase your pedaling speed by about 40 percent, according to expert bikers. How? By allowing you to pull up with one pedal while you're pushing down with the other one.

Toe clips are great for racing pros and very experienced cyclists who ride long distances on the open road. But the problem with toe clips is that in order to get any benefit from them, the straps must be tightened enough so that your foot won't accidentally slip out. And then, guess what? You can't get your foot out quickly, even if you need to. In an emergency, toe clips can be *very dangerous*.

On city streets or any place where there are a lot of lights or traffic, toe clips just aren't a good idea. If you're going on a long-distance tour on country roads, you may want to try toe clips. In that case, have an experienced rider show you how to get them on and off quickly. There's a trick to it, and you'll need to practice before using them on the road.

GLOVES

Padded biking gloves do three things for your hands. They take some of the pressure off your nerves during a long ride. They protect your hands from scrapes if you fall. And they protect your hands when you have to do simple work on your bike, such as changing a tire.

ELBOW PADS AND KNEE PADS

These are a good idea if you are into BMX racing or freestyle. Any kind of hard plastic pads will do—soccer pads or hockey pads, for instance. Biking stores may not carry them, so check the sporting goods section of a discount store.

CARRIERS AND PANNIERS

In the old days, you had to carry your gear in a wire basket on the front of your bike. Now you can get sleek pouches or saddle bags called panniers (pan-y-ers). The panniers are attached to aluminum carriers that are mounted on the front or back of your bike.

Make sure you load panniers evenly, otherwise

you'll be off-balance. And remember that the added weight of packages or panniers will make steering and handling your bike a little more difficult. Practice riding with a full load before going out into traffic.

Even without panniers, you can strap a small package to a bike carrier, or get a seat bag or handlebar bag. These bike pouches are excellent for carrying the small things that you need. For really small things, like money, keys and pressure gauge, you might want to use one of the "bum bags" or waist packs that you strap around your waist.

ODOMETERS

A speedometer measures your speed, but an odometer measures the distance you've traveled. Your parents probably have an odometer on their car, counting up the miles. Odometers are great when you're riding a certain number of miles and want to check and see how far you've already gone.

Cycling odometers are about the size of a pack of gum. You can mount one on the front fork, and it will count the revolutions of the front wheel. How? There's a little arm that sticks out, and every time a spoke passes the arm, it moves the counter ahead. It also makes a twanging sound. Some people are driven crazy by the noise. Others think it's a totally awesome effect—as good as those colored beads and springs that you can add to your bike to make a clicking sound.

KICKSTANDS

Most biking pros will tell you to forget about kickstands. They say kickstands add extra weight to your bike and can add wind resistance too. But, hey—if you're riding a standard 20-inch kids' bike, it already weighs about 30 pounds anyway! Kids' bikes are not made of the super-lightweight materials and construction that you find on road bikes. So what's the harm in adding a few more ounces for a kickstand? If you want a kickstand, go for it. If you have a derailleur system, a kickstand is actually a really good idea.

Expensive adult bikes, on the other hand, are better off without kickstands. Here's why. When you use a kickstand, you tend to think the bike is okay—that it won't fall over. But lightweight bikes can be knocked over easily. They can even blow over in the wind. And when a lightweight bike falls, a lot of delicate parts can get bent. So when you get a lightweight bike, it's best to do without a kickstand and find a good solid place to lean the bike instead.

Important note: Some people will tell you just to go ahead and lay your bike down on the ground. Fine. But never lay it on the bike's right side. You can bend the derailleur out of shape.

LIGHTS

This is a touchy subject because bicycle lights are really cool, but they're for one thing and one thing only: riding at night. And you just shouldn't be riding your bike at night. Why not? Because night riding is dangerous for a zillion reasons. For one thing, you can't see the road as well so you're more likely to hit a pothole or miss a turn. But more important, you can't be seen very well by motorists. You might think your bike shines like a Ferris wheel with all the reflectors and lights you put on it, but motorists have a very hard time seeing bikers at night—especially if the motorists are traveling fast. They can't see you as quickly or as well as you can see them because the lights on your bicycle aren't as bright as the lights on their car. There is no good reason for you to take that kind of risk, so stay off the street at night. Period!

If you're truly determined to buy a bike light, be aware that bike lights present a lot of problems. They're heavy, and the battery-operated ones tend to fail when you need them the most. If you take a spill on your bike, your light can get broken or smashed. Even if you don't fall, it can be stolen while your bike is parked somewhere.

The best headlights use quartz halogen bulbs and batteries—regular or rechargeable. You'll need a taillight too, if you're really going to ride after dark. Some people remove the standard taillight bulbs and replace them with halogen bulbs to make them more visible on the road.

As an alternative to a headlight, you might consider buying a flashlight with a handlebar mount. The mount, or clamp, stays on your bike all the time. The flashlight slips in and out. That way, if you want to hop off your bike and hike

WHEEL FACTS

- Racers who train at high altitudes have an advantage in racing. That's one reason our Olympic team trains in Colorado Springs, Colorado, which has an elevation of 6,200 feet above sea level.

through the woods, you can take your light with you.

Don't let anyone talk you into buying a light set with a generator system. These lights sound really cool because they work on pedal power. No batteries included—or required! As you pedal your bike, the generator takes energy from your front wheel and causes the light to shine. But as soon as you slow down, the light starts to grow dimmer. When you stop, you're left standing in the dark. Worst of all, the generator puts a lot of drag on the front wheel, making it much harder to pedal.

There is one other high-tech and dazzling accessory you might want—for safety's sake and for the plain fun of it. It's a set of micro-prism reflectors. If you find yourself riding home when it's starting to get dark, these reflectors will help make your bicycle more visible to other vehicles on the road. They are much more effective than the reflectors that come with your bike, and lightweight, too. These reflectors usually come in a kit of 20 self-adhesive strips which you apply to the rims of your wheels. They create a fabulous effect, shimmering as you zip down the road, and they can be seen from hundreds of yards away.

WHISTLES, SIRENS AND BELLS

"BEEEEP! Look out! Get out of my way or we're going to crash!" That's basically what a whistle, bell or siren says. Some cyclists are foolish enough to blow their whistles and whiz through red lights, sure that motorists and pedestrians will hear them and immediately clear the way. Needless to say, that's a rude habit and a dangerous one as well. If you follow the rules of the road, you won't need a

bell or whistle most of the time. And the few times when you might need it—when a motorist doesn't see you and is veering dangerously close, for example—the whistle or bell won't do you much good. By the time you reach for the bell, you could more easily have swerved your bike out of danger's way.

On the other hand, you might want a siren just for the fun of it—to announce your arrival in your friend's driveway, for instance. Sirens, bells and horns just for the fun of it? Sure! What else are bicycles for if not to have fun?

CUSTOMIZED EXTRAS

Aerobars, gel seats (those comfortable seats made of thick, squishy gel), mirrors, handlebar grips with streamers and without! There are dozens of parts on your bike that you can replace with fancy extras or spice up with something colorful. Chances are you don't really need any of these things, but since most of them can be removed and put on your new bike when you grow out of the old one, it might be fun to consider some of these extras. Your best bet is to buy special gear from a bike shop and talk to a salesperson about the different choices. Remember, though: Customized extras don't always make biking easier. For instance, aerobars do make you go faster, but they also make it more difficult to steer.

DO-IT-YOURSELF CUSTOMIZING

One of the best ways to attract attention on the road, at a race or at school is to show up with a custom-painted bike. An old bike can suddenly look fantastic with a splatter paint job, a two-tone or some stenciled designs. You can even get new colored hand grips or bicycle seats to match and neon colored tape to wrap around the handlebars.

The important thing about painting your bike is to be sure you don't get *any* paint inside the moving parts. For instance, you can't get paint anywhere near the handlebar stem because it can drip inside and ruin the bearings. The best way to paint your bike is to take it apart first—totally! Remove the handlebars, saddle, wheels, cranks, pedals, chain, freewheel—everything. Strip it down to the frame! Then you can spray paint it, or splatter paint it, without fear. Use automobile paint. Plan your paint job at a time when your bike needs a tune-up (if it's a multi-speed bike). Then you can pay a bike shop to put it back together for you, and tune it up at the same time.

You might also want to jazz up your bike with reflective tape—making patterns on the fenders or the down tube, for instance. Use two colors of tape for a fabulous optical effect. Check with an adult about the kind of tape you're planning to use, however. Some kinds of tape are so sticky, they could goop up your bike frame if you have to remove them.

What else can you do to make your bike unique? The answer is easy: seat covers! Many bike shops sell seat covers in various colors and designs. Or if you or someone you know can sew, you can have a custom seat cover made. It's easy to take a piece of fabric and some elastic and

WHEEL FACTS

- **Tiffany's, the famous New York jewelry store, made a bicycle out of precious metals and gems in the 1890s. The frame was silver (real silver!); the handles were ivory and jade; and the lights were ruby and crystal. A wealthy Englishman bought it the day after it appeared in the store.**

transform them into a radical seat cover—maybe even using an old pair of jeans. If you use the "seat" of the pants with the pocket still attached, you'll have an instant hiding place on your bike to store phone numbers, small change or even a spare key.

CHAPTER 5

WILD WHEELS!

Hold on to your gear shift levers. Here come some of the weirdest, wildest and wackiest wheels you've ever seen! From the early days of bicycling to the technical triumphs of tomorrow, these bikes take you on a tour of the human imagination! Just wait till you see what can be done with two wheels and a few pounds of steel.

It was called a lot of things, including the Ordinary. But there was nothing ordinary about the scrapes and bruises you could get when you fell off this bicycle. Riders were told to head for the bushes if they felt that they were losing control. Even getting on was difficult. You had to climb up from a fence or a special set of steps. Ordinaries became popular in the 1870s; this photograph was taken in 1881.

No one ever said learning to ride was easy! In the late 1860s these bicycles, which were called velocipedes, were so hard to ride that New York City had its own velocipede riding school. This is a scene from one of its classes. Thank goodness bike designs have improved —and you don't have to go to a school like this!

Many of the earliest bikes, like this British velocipede—which was built in 1827—didn't have pedals. The rider had to run along the ground to propel it!

The Ordinary may have been a challenge to ride, but that didn't stop these brave cyclists from holding a twenty-five mile race. These riders could have definitely used helmets!

A bicycle built for ten? This bicycle is a marvel of frame design and drive-train engineering. Look at how the chain rings increase in size: The "monster" chain ring at the very back of the bike transfers the power of all ten riders to the rear wheel. But watch out for sharp turns!

This is one of the earliest bicycles built for two. Made in the late 1800s, it was called the Sociable. On today's tandems one rider sits behind the other, but on this bike they sat side by side—which made things, well … sociable!

Recumbent bikes may look strange, but they're actually very efficient. The long wheel base and stretched-out riding position make riding more comfortable than it is on a traditional "upright" bike. Some people say these bikes are the wave of the future.

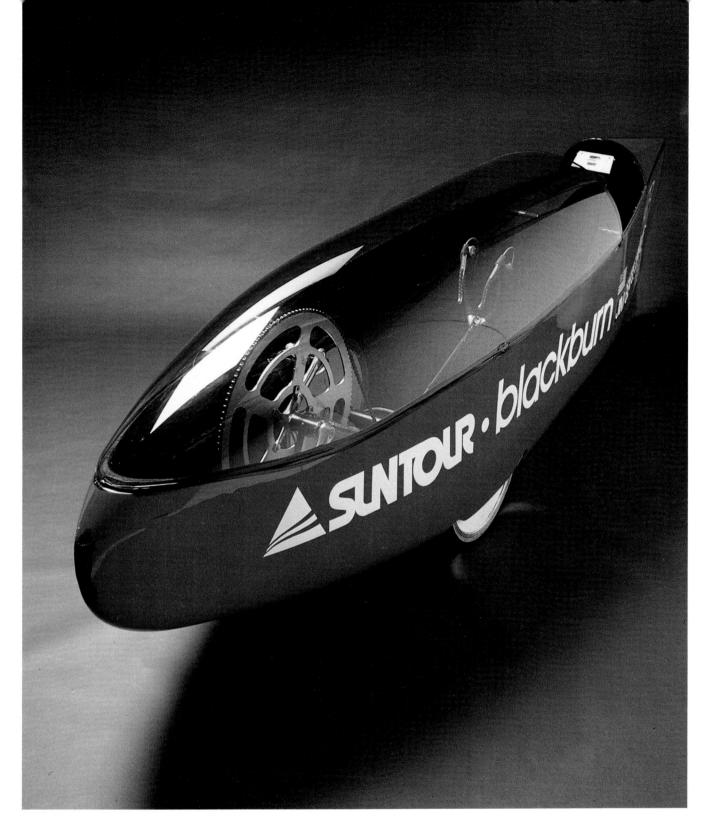

If this 1981 Suntour looks more like a racing car than a bike, that's because it too was built for speed. The wheels, pedals and gears are all inside a shell that cuts down on wind resistance.

This three-wheel recumbent has an extra energy source: the sun. On this solar-powered bicycle, solar collectors on the top and front of the bike give the rider an extra boost—unless it's raining!

The Gold Rush. This bike won an $18,000 prize for being the first human-powered vehicle on land to break the 65 miles per hour speed limit. The rider, Fast Freddy Markham, pedaled 65.484 miles per hour with no tail wind and no pace car—and this 1986 recumbent bicycle went to the Smithsonian Museum. That's Fast Freddy inside and bike designer Gardner Martin behind him.

Here's a bike that raced in the 1988 Olympics. It has disk wheels (no spokes), a front wheel that's smaller than its back wheel, and forward-reaching handlebars. All these features help reduce the bike's wind resistance. The rider's crouch, tightly fitting clothes and helmet help too.

TUNE-UPS & TOTAL REPAIRS

Bike adjustments and repairs fall into three basic categories. First there's the stuff anyone can do with a little training. Changing a tire, raising or lowering the seat and adding some grease to the chain all fall into that category. Then there are trickier adjustments—tightening a brake cable or fixing a derailleur that doesn't want to derail properly. Before you start, you need to know what's easy, what's hard and what to do about both. You also should know how to deal with a bike shop.

TOOLS

Before you even think about working on your bike, you've got to have the right tools. Don't try to change a tire without tire irons, for instance. You can damage your bike even further, or totally destroy some of the more delicate parts, by using the wrong tools. These are the basics:

- 3 tire irons
- 2 6-inch adjustable crescent wrenches
- small screwdriver
- tire patch kit
- tire pump and pressure gauge
- gloves to protect your hands

PUMPING UP YOUR TIRES

The best way to protect your tires from damage and prevent flats is to keep them properly inflated. If you do this, you may never have to read the next section on how to fix a flat tire. Under-inflated tires are the most common cause of punctures on kids' bikes. When your tires are low and you ride over a curb or other large object, the tire is pressed against the rim. The rim cuts into the tube, making small holes. Bike shop people call these holes "snake bites."

Filling your tires with air is easy and trouble free if you follow a few simple rules.

- Never fill a bicycle tire with air from a gas station pump. The pressure is too high, and your tires can explode. Always use a hand or foot bicycle pump instead.

- Inflate your tires to the correct pressure. It's usually printed on the side of the tire. An average pressure for many knobby tires is 35psi, or pounds per square inch. But find out for sure about your own bike! If you're smaller than average, however, you can use a little less than the recommended amount of air. If you're much bigger or heavier than average, you need even more air in your tires than the recommended amount.

- On a hot day, use two or three pounds less air. This might mean you have to let some air out. The air in the tires will expand as it heats and could cause a blowout.

FIXING A FLAT

If you do get a flat, you can probably repair it yourself. Bicycles aren't like cars—you don't carry a spare bicycle tire, do you? Instead of replacing a flat tire with a new one, you take the tire off, patch it and then put it back on. It's a fairly simple repair job. But as with any kind of repair work, it's a whole lot easier to do it yourself after you've seen someone else do it once. You might want to ask an adult for help or take your bike to a bike shop the first time you get a flat. It also helps to have an extra pair of hands when you're removing and replacing the wheel. Here are step-by-step instructions for your second flat tire or—if you're brave—your first!

BEFORE YOU BEGIN:
Check the valve stem on the flat tire to see if it's leaking. Why? Because if it's a leak and not a puncture, there's no point in removing the tire. Here's the leak test: Remove the valve cap and put a small blob of spit on the stem. If air is escaping, it will cause the spit to bubble up a little bit. Pump up the tire and replace the valve cap. Tighten the cap. If the tire goes flat again soon, look for a puncture. You may have a hole *and* a leaky stem! Or you may have a defective valve, in which case you'll need a new tire.

STEP 1—REMOVING THE WHEEL:
Turn your bike upside down and balance it on the seat and handlebars.

If the flat is on a front wheel, use two wrenches, one on each side, to loosen the nuts. With both wrenches in position, twist them at the same time, in opposite directions. (Both nuts will be turning counterclockwise. But since they are on opposite sides of the wheel, they seem to move in opposite directions.) Remove the nuts, bolts and washers. Be sure to remember where the washers are, and put them back in the same position when you're finished fixing the tire. Now go on to Step 2.

If the flat is on a back wheel with a derailleur, it's a little harder to remove the tire. First, shift

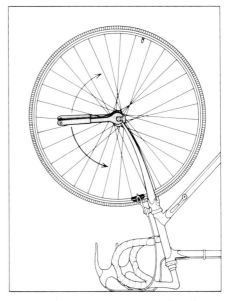

To remove the front wheel, use two wrenches (make sure they turn in opposite directions) to first loosen the nuts.

gears (if necessary) to get the chain onto the smallest freewheel sprocket. Remember to keep the pedals moving while shifting. You may have to pedal by hand, with a friend lifting the bike, and then shift. Now use your fingers to remove the chain from the freewheel altogether. Another way to say this is that the chain cannot be resting on the sprockets or cogs—the gears—because those gears are actually attached to the wheel. When you pull the wheel out, the gears are going to come with it. The chain must stay on the bike. So you have to move the chain off the gears. It can stay in the derailleur system, though.

Now you're ready to remove the rear wheel. Use two wrenches to remove the nuts, following the instructions for a front wheel. When the nuts and bolts are off, you'll have to gently push the derailleur out of the way—otherwise the wheel won't come out. When the wheel is off, go on to Step 2.

STEP 2—REMOVING THE TIRE:
Find a flat surface to work on.

Inspect the tire and try to find the leak. If there is a piece of glass, remove it carefully. Then let all the air out of the tire. You might have to press on the pin in the middle of the stem with a small screwdriver to get the rest of the air out.

Now you're going to remove two parts: the tire and the tube that's inside the tire. It's a two-step process. First you loosen the tire enough to pull the tube out. Then you take the tire the rest of the way off.

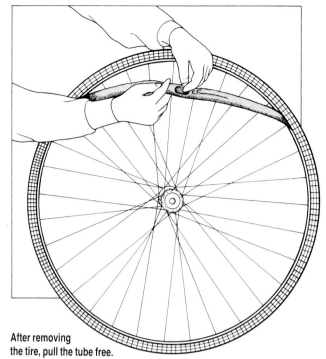

After removing
the tire, pull the tube free.

To remove the tire, start on the edge opposite the valve. Insert one tire iron between the tire and the rim. It should go in with the flat side down, the tapered side up. Try to pry the bead, or edge of the tire, loose. The bead is really a wire inside the edge, and you don't want to tear or damage it, so don't use a lot of force.

If the tire won't come loose, use two tire irons. Leave the first one inserted under the rim. To keep it in place, hook it under a spoke, as shown in the illustration. Then, three or four inches away, insert a second tire iron. Try not to puncture the tube, which is inside the tire, with the tire irons. You might even have to use a third iron, several inches away from the first two. When one side of the tire is completely loosened, you should be able to pull most of the tube out from under the tire. But you won't be able to pull the valve out yet. Continue loosening the tire, and when it is completely free, remove the tube—valve and all.

STEP 3—FINDING THE HOLE: Now you can patch the puncture in the tube. But where is it? To find it, fill a bucket or sink with water. Pump air back into the tube. Put the tube under water and watch for bubbles. The bubbles indicate escaping air—that's where the leak is! Take the tube out of the water and use a piece of chalk to mark the location of the hole.

If you're out on the road without a bucket (and most people are!) you'll have to find the leak another way. Fully inflate the tube and hold it next to your cheek. Listen for a hissing noise, or try to feel the air escaping.

STEP 4—PATCHING: The patch kit you bought will most likely come with instructions. Follow them. The steps are basically 1) use sandpaper to sand the area that needs to be patched, 2) apply rubber cement, 3) cut a patch to fit the area and 4) press the patch in place. All this is done with the tube deflated, of course.

STEP 5—INVESTIGATE: Now that you've mended the tube, try to find out what caused the flat. Was it a piece of glass or a tack stuck in the tire? If so, remove it. You may need to inspect the inside of the tire to find the sharp object, but do it carefully. Don't run your fingers around inside the tire—you might cut yourself. Use your eyes instead. If you can't find a piece of glass or a nail, consider this possibility: One of your spokes may have caused the puncture. There's a rubber strip that should prevent the spokes from poking the tube. Look for it, and make sure it's doing its job.

STEP 6—REPLACING THE TIRE: Now it's time to pump some air into the tube again. Pump it

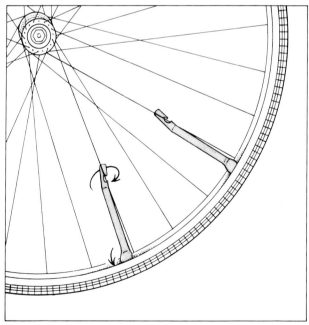

To lift the tire from the rim, insert the first tire iron under the rim and hold it in place by hooking it around a spoke. Then insert the second one three to four inches away.

half-full of air. Then stick the valve back through the hole in the rim. Don't pull it tight yet. Position the tube around the rim, the way it should go. Begin trying to fit the tire over the tube, being careful not to pinch the tube between the bead and the rim. The beaded edge of the tire must go back on the rim the way it was before you removed it. Be patient—this is the hardest part of the job. You might have to use tire irons to help the bead over the edge, but do so carefully. At this point, it's easy to mangle your rims or puncture the tube all over again!

When the tire is completely replaced on the rim, pump it back up to full pressure.

If the flat tire was on a front wheel, just put it back on the bike. Remember to replace the washers with the bolts and nuts. Tighten both nuts at the same time, turning the wrenches in opposite directions the way you did when you removed the wheel.

For a rear wheel with derailleur, you'll have to position the axle in the dropouts. (Dropouts are the holes at the end of the fork and the end of the seatstays.) Then replace the chain on the smallest freewheel sprocket. Pull the wheel all the way back to the back of the dropout slots. Then straighten the axle in the frame and tighten the nuts and bolts.

ADJUSTING THE SADDLE HEIGHT

As you grow, you will have to move your seat up so that your legs are fully extended when you

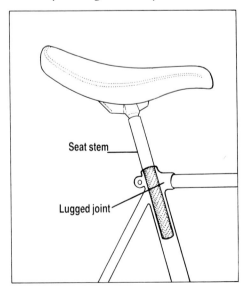

Seat stem

Lugged joint

Leaving 2 to 2½ inches of seat stem inside the seat tube

pedal. There are two rules about adjusting the saddle, though. One is that you must *always* leave at least 2 to 2½ inches of seat stem inside the seat tube. Look for a line on the stem indicating the maximum height. If you can't find it, take the seat *all the way out* of the seat tube so you can measure it, and mark the 2½-inch length yourself. That's the amount of stem that must remain inside the seat tube for safety.

The other rule about seat height adjustments is that you must be sure to tighten the binder bolts securely when you're done. Use two wrenches, one on each side of the clamp, and twist in opposite directions.

Remember that when you raise the saddle, you put yourself farther away from the handlebars. On some bikes you can raise the handlebars. But be twice as cautious about tightening the binder bolts if you do! Loose handlebars are even more dangerous than a loose seat.

ALL ABOUT CHAINS

On a single-speed bike, such as a BMX bike, there isn't much you need to do to your chain. To be safe, a chain should be able to move up and down no more than half an inch. That's called having half-inch play in it. If the chain seems loose to you, have it looked at by a bike-shop technician. The danger is that the chain can come off while you're riding. When that happens, you will lose control of your bike and you might crash.

If your chain starts to get rusty, spray it with a Teflon lubricant. That will slow down the rusting process, but it won't remove the rust. If the rust is so thick that the chain isn't moving, you'll need a new one. Go to a bike shop and have them replace it for you.

Multispeed bikes with derailleurs are a different story, however. These chains need to be cleaned and relubricated regularly—about every three months. Your chain may get dirty even faster if you ride in dusty areas or put a lot of miles on your bike. Removing the chain is simple with a chain-link remover. Then you soak the chain in kerosene and scrub it with an old toothbrush to get the gunk off. But again, this is a job you'll learn faster and more easily if you watch someone do it first. When you take your bike in for a

WHEEL FACTS

- **The Ordinary bike is making a comeback. Mike Rust of Salida, California, has started making his own high-wheelers. He and his brothers ride them down the mountain trails to the amazement of local residents.**

tune-up, ask the bike-shop technician to show you how it's done. Then next time you'll be able to do it yourself.

BRAKE ADJUSTMENTS

If you have coaster brakes, you can skip this section. There aren't any adjustments you can make to your coaster brakes, and you shouldn't need to.

Caliper brakes are different. The brake cable that controls a caliper brake can stretch—and does stretch—in normal use. It will need to be tightened from time to time. To find out if your brakes need to be tightened, squeeze the brake levers as hard as you can. There should still be a space between the lever and the handlebar—at least one inch. If the clearance is less than one inch, your brake cables need an adjustment.

To tighten the cable, look for a pair of small rings at one end of the cable or the other. They may be near the wheel or near the brake levers. One of the rings is a locknut. You'll recognize it by its six or eight sides—like the other nuts on your bike. The other ring has ridges (called threads), like the top of a tube of toothpaste. That's so you can grip it and turn it. Loosen the locknut with pliers. Then turn the adjustment ring until the cable is tightened.

How much should you tighten it? Look at the brake shoes. There should be a 3/32-inch clearance between each brake shoe and each rim. If you have turned the adjusting barrel as far as it will go, and the brake shoes still aren't close enough to the rim, you need an adjustment that will shorten the cable. Ask a bike shop technician for help. You can learn to do it, but it's not something you should learn from a book. Get some hands-on help and you'll soon be a real pro!

BIKE SHOP REPAIRS: WHAT TO EXPECT

Most bike shop people love bikes and are happy to help riders learn about their bikes. They are basically an honest bunch of people, too. Most of them will tell you the truth about what your bike needs and give you good advice about repairs.

If you buy a bike at a bike shop, you should be able to bring it in for a free tune-up sometime within the first few months after purchase. You should also be able to ask questions about adjustments, and have simple adjustments made, even beyond the 30-day tune-up period. For instance, if your brake cables need an adjustment, the bike shop will probably help you do it or show you how to do it for free.

What's a bike tune-up, and do you need one? A tune-up is a thorough cleaning, checking and adjusting of all bike parts. In 1989 the average cost of a tune-up was $30 for a multispeed bike. If your bike has a derailleur and hand brakes, you need to have it tuned. You probably need a tune-up when you buy it to make sure everything is adjusted from the start. After that, you need a tune-up twice a year.

If you buy a used bike or a new bike that didn't come with a free tune-up, you can still get it checked out in a bike shop, but you'll have to pay for the service.

If your bike is a single-speed BMX or cruiser, forget about tuning it up. Single-speed bikes need very little attention. Spray the chain with a lubricant to keep it working smoothly and keep your tires inflated. That's about all a basic bike needs.

SHOW-OFF SMART-OFF QUIZ

Think you're an expert on cycling? Here's your chance to show off how much you know—or learn some fascinating facts that you can smart off to your friends!

1. An average adult man will eat about 2,200 calories per day. How many calories per day do bicycle racers consume each day of a marathon?
   a) 1,000 calories
   b) 20,000 calories
   c) 6,000 calories

2. There is a road race that cyclists call the "Tour of the Moon." Where is it held?
   a) at the North Pole
   b) straight across Siberia and back
   c) around the Colorado National Monument

3. To cut down on wind resistance, some professional bicycle racers will
   a) shave all the hair on their bodies
   b) close their eyes while riding
   c) ride with one arm strapped to their stomachs

4. Which of these materials is *not* being used in the newest high-tech bicycle frames?
   a) titanium
   b) uranium
   c) magnesium

5. During the Tour de France, bicycle mechanics travel with the racers and spend three to six hours working on the bikes each night. Where do they do this work?
   a) in hotel ballrooms
   b) on the street or sidewalk
   c) in hotel bathtubs
   d) all of the above

6. At a school in Newberry, Ohio, every single student
   a) rides a bicycle to the prom
   b) learns how to ride a unicycle and rides one in class
   c) is on the U.S. Olympic cycling team

d) paints his or her bicycle with the school colors

7. In the 1800s, the old-fashioned bicycles with huge front wheels were called penny-farthings. Why?
   a) Because they cost between a penny and a farthing to buy.
   b) They were invented by a man named Farthing, who named the bicycle for his daughter, Penny.
   c) The front wheel looked like a big English penny compared to the rear wheel, which looked like a small farthing coin.

8. Which country is estimated to have the largest number of bicycles?
   a) United States
   b) China
   c) India
   d) France

9. In 1981-82, David Duncan and three other cyclists biked around the world on 18-speed bikes. They took all kinds of supplies with them, including foreign language guides, rabies vaccines and shortwave radios. But they didn't anticipate they would *each* have to deal with
   a) getting a bad case of the chicken pox
   b) having 100 flat ties
   c) being mistaken for spies

10. The world's record for bicycle balancing, according to the *Guinness Book of World Records,* is 24 hours and 6 minutes. What is bicycle balancing?
   a) balancing a bicycle on your head or nose
   b) riding a bicycle without holding on to the handlebars
   c) balancing on a bicycle without rolling forward or backward, and without touching a foot to the ground

Answers on page 79.

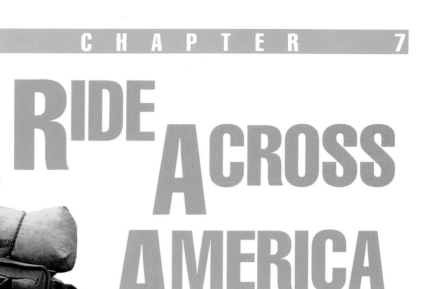

CHAPTER 7

RIDE ACROSS AMERICA

Think about this: There are more than 88 million people in America who own or ride bikes. But only a million of them ever use their bikes to go on tours or vacations. Touring is taking a long bike ride—a ride that lasts anywhere from one day to several weeks or a year or more.

So why aren't more people touring?

The answer is probably that not all 88 million people are in shape for a long-distance bicycle tour. Touring takes strength and stamina—the ability to keep going. You'll be riding for many hours at a time, and you need to know how to repair your bike if it breaks down. And touring takes guts. It's kind of like being a pioneer, heading out across America in a covered wagon—except that the pioneers had horses to pull the load, and they could go inside their wagons when it rained!

But that's what makes touring such an adventure. It's an experience for those who dare! And there are lots of ways to get into bicycle touring without facing the hardships of the original Oregon Trail. You can enjoy the excitement of bicycle touring on a small scale, even if you're a beginner. If other family members own bikes, you can start learning how to tour right away.

TOURING FOR BEGINNERS

The key to learning about bicycle touring is to start small. Never take on more than you're ready for, both in terms of experience and physical condition. Make your first bicycle tour a one-day ride in the country, or even a half-day ride around town. That way, if your bike breaks down, you get too tired, or you find that you've brought all the wrong stuff with you, it won't matter. You won't be far from home.

Of course, if you want to be able to call home for help, someone should be there to answer the call. So when you take your first tour, try to do it when someone is at home who can come rescue you in the car. Ninety-nine times out of a hundred, you'll have a great ride and the person who stayed home will have nothing to do except pout about being left behind. But it's good to have a "safety net" the first time you go on a long ride.

After your first all-day tour, you'll probably know a whole lot more about how to plan a bicycle tour. You'll know what to pack and what

You can go almost anywhere on the right bike! These cyclists are in Red Rock Canyon, Nevada.

WHEEL FACTS

- **The world's longest bicycle is a tandem that weighs as much as a car—2,425 pounds—and seats 35 riders. The monster bike is a dangerous machine and is very difficult to stop. And ouch! At over a ton, it's heavy when it falls on you!**

to leave behind, how to dress, how much money to bring, how often you'll need to stop for more water—and you'll know how much fun bicycle touring is! The sheer thrill of being out on the road, wandering at will, seeing the sights or going nowhere but setting your own pace—it's a fantastic way to spend the day. Invite a friend along to share the fun. Soon you'll be ready to plan more advanced trips.

WHAT TO PACK FOR A ONE-DAY TOUR

- Water bottle
- One or two spare tires
- Tool kit containing Crescent wrench, tire irons, screwdriver and pliers
- Tire patch kit
- Pump and pressure gauge
- Rain poncho or cape
- Bike lock
- Maps and compass
- Money, including small change for telephone calls
- ID, so that in case of emergency, people will know who you are

Optional:
- Sun block (important on hot, sunny days)
- Insect repellent
- Sunglasses, to keep the glare and bugs out of your eyes
- Small first-aid kit with bandages and first-aid cream
- Plastic garbage bag (to put garbage in, keep wet things in, etc.)
- Lunch or enough money to buy meals
- Duct tape for emergency repairs

AFTER YOUR FIRST TOUR

If you survived your first bicycle tour, you're probably ready for another trip. You may even want to try an overnight trip. But be realistic. If you've never gone camping before, you're probably not ready to pack a bunch of gear onto a bike and ride off into the sunset. And if you're not too swift on medium-sized hills, you probably don't want to head off for a tour of the Rockies. In other words, choose a longer tour that you and your companions can really handle.

For most people, the *best* bicycle tours are the ones that are close to home—a tour in your own state or a closely neighboring state. Why? Mainly because you're more likely to go on a bike tour if you don't have to travel a great distance to do it. There are probably areas you've always wanted to explore within a few hundred miles of your house. For inspiration, write to your state's Department of Parks and Recreation and your state's Office of Tourism. They'll send you free information, brochures and, best of all, bicycle maps. If your family does a lot of touring, you may want to contact one of the bicycling organizations in the Appendix to find out about tours far from home.

There are several ways to take longer bicycle tours while you're still somewhat inexperienced. Two suggestions are listed below.

PACKAGE BICYCLE TOURS

Package tours are led by professionals who know the roads. They plan the route and arrange for a van to follow along with your gear, so you don't have to carry the extra load. They also provide the food and find good campgrounds. The fee you pay for joining the tour also includes the use of their mechanic on the trip if something goes wrong with your bike. It's a worry-free way to hit the open roads, and you'll learn a lot in the process. If you've never patched a flat tire, for instance, you'll probably get the chance to watch an expert do it right.

For more information about package tours, check the classified ads in bicycling magazines, ask at your local bike shop or contact a biking organization such as American Youth Hostels,

Bikecentennial or Sierra Club. Bikecentennial not only sponsors tours, but they also sell a guide to bike vacations that costs about $2. It lists 150 different tour operators in the U.S. and abroad, with prices and trip destinations. Addresses for Bikecennial and AYH are listed in the Appendix.

AMERICAN YOUTH HOSTELS

Wouldn't it be great to stay in a hotel where most of the guests arrive on their own power—on foot, by bicycle or by canoe? That's sort of what a youth hostel is—a no-frills place to stay for hikers, bikers and other travelers. You can join an AYH package tour, or you can stay at the hostels on your own, as an individual traveler. Either way, you'll have a unique experience, one that you're guaranteed not to forget.

Hostels are really more like college dormitories than hotels. You can't get room service, and you have to bring your own food, towels and sheets. But so what? You can't beat the price. Hostels charge as little as five dollars a night! You sleep indoors, so you're always warm and dry no matter what the weather. And some hostels are located in exciting, unusual places—in a lighthouse in California, for instance!

If you're interested in taking low-cost overnight bicycle trips, consider joining American Youth Hostels. Membership is open to adults and kids for a small fee (about $10 for kids 17 and under). With your membership, you'll get a handbook listing and describing the 200 hostels in the United States as well as an ID card. If you want to stay at a hostel, you must be a member of AYH and show your ID card. To join, write or call Ameican Youth Hotels in Washington, D.C. (See the Appendix for the address.)

WHAT TO PACK FOR A LONGER TRIP

What do you need on an overnight bicycle trip? Your Nintendo Gameboy? Five pounds of trail mix? Clean clothes for each day you'll be gone? No, no, and *no way*. Rule Number 1 for bicycle touring is: Travel light. No matter how much you like your Gameboy, when you're pedaling up a hill with a fully loaded bike, you're going to wish you'd left half of your gear at home.

Exactly what gear to take depends on how long you'll be traveling, where you're going to sleep, what the weather is like along your route, who's going with you and your level of experience. For instance, should you take extra links for your bike chain? That's a great idea—*if* you know how to maintain and repair your bike. But if you've never removed a bike chain, the chances are that you're not going to learn how in the middle of a country road. How about a tent? Should you take one along? Not if you're planning to sleep at a friend's house, in a motel or in a hostel. As you can see, each trip is different and the list of gear for each trip varies, too.

In general, don't worry about packing food. Instead be prepared to buy food each evening, right before you stop for the night. Buy just enough for that night's dinner and breakfast the next morning. Plan to pick up lunch each day at a carry-out or restaurant along the way.

You may also want a snack for later. Some trail mix, a piece of fruit or perhaps a muffin or bagel are all good bike snacks. So is some sort of granola bar that's *not* made with sugar. The reason to avoid sugar when biking is that sugar gives you a shot of instant energy that burns off almost immediately—making you feel even more tired when the "sugar high" is gone. If you want steady energy for a long ride, make sure you eat lots of complex carbohydrates, such as rice, cereal, pasta, potatoes and corn.

The rule about what to take along is this: Take the gear you think you'll need, no more and no less. Try to keep your load of gear to 15 pounds if you're under 14 years old, 30 pounds maximum for older teenagers and adults. It's a good idea to weigh your fully packed bags on the bathroom scale *before* setting off. And remember to pack the heaviest items on the bottom of your bags. You don't want a lot of weight on top that might tip your balance.

The following is a list of gear, some of which you might not think to take. It's *not* a complete list, but these things can be handy.

- All the gear listed under "What to Pack for a One-Day Tour."
- Pocket knife

• More plastic bags (useful for keeping everything dry in a rainstorm, for storing garbage, for keeping clothes separate, etc.

• Survival manual—if you're planning to camp, there's a lot to know about the wilderness. For instance, experienced campers in places like Maine and the Sierras usually put *all* their food, *and* the clothes worn while cooking the food, in a plastic bag. Then they hang the plastic bag in a tree *far* from the campsite. Why? Bears! Anything that smells like food can attract bears to your campsite. Read a good book about camping before you sleep outdoors for the first time, and take a small survival manual along on your camping/cycling tour.

• Special bicycle maps showing topographical details—namely hills! It's always nice to know ahead of time when you're going to have to pedal up Mt. Everest. Bike maps can be obtained from state parks departments or the Department of Transportation. They are also available from AYH and Bikecentennial. (See the Appendix.)

• Small flashlight with halogen bulb

• Camera and film

TOTAL TRAINING—GETTING INTO SHAPE FOR A TOUR

Getting into shape is simply a matter of starting with short rides and working up to longer ones. At first, try a 30-minute ride with no stops—except for traffic, stop signs and lights, of course. Then work up to a one-hour ride. Be sure to drink some water every 10 to 15 minutes.

Try to keep your legs moving at about the same pace the whole time. This will be almost

Packed with panniers on both the front and rear wheels, and a sleeping bag on the back rack, this bike is ready for some serious touring along the Oregon coast.

impossible unless your bike has high and low gears. With gears, the idea is to shift gears whenever you need to in order to maintain the same pace or *cadence*. Adults who are in fair-to-good shape can maintain a pace of 70 revolutions of the pedals per minute, called 70rpm. When you come to a hill, shift to a lower gear so that your legs don't pedal any slower. Going downhill, shift to a high gear and *keep pedaling*. Use common sense, however. You can't keep pedaling downhill if the hill is steep and you're using your brakes the whole way.

As soon as you can ride for one solid hour without tiring, you are in good shape to take a longer ride. Double your touring time to two hours and see how you feel. Take a short rest at least once during the two-hour ride, but don't stop exercising suddenly. Cooling down slowly is an important part of any exercise program.

If you're going on an overnight tour, it's a good idea to take practice rides with fully-packed saddlebags. That way you'll be used to riding with the extra weight.

Even if you've had lots of practice, don't think that you can ride all day at 70rpm. Unless you're a world-class athlete, you'll have to set a slower pace and stop to rest several times. Also, don't make the mistake of trying to build muscles by using high gears—the ones that are harder to pedal. It puts too much strain on your knees, and you can actually cause an injury.

Most important, remember that it's better for your body if you don't push *too* hard. Take your physical training one step at a time. If you do it right, touring will develop muscle, stamina and strength!

So you don't have a camel...

BICYCLING'S BEST

Fastest time in the Race Across America (RAAM) marathon: A new record, set in 1989 by 35-year-old Paul Solon of Tiburon, California. He almost dropped out of the race because of neck injuries, but hung in there and won first place by crossing the finish line in 8 days, 8 hours and 45 minutes.

Fastest woman cyclist: Jeannie Longo of France. In 1987, she won three major championships: the Tour Feminin (women's Tour de France), the Coors Classic and the World Road Championship. In 1986, she set three women's world records, within three months, for going the greatest distance in 60 minutes, both indoors and out. Each record was for riding more than 27 miles in an hour.

Most famous cyclist: Eddie Merckx of Belgium, who won the Tour de France five times. Merckx also won the triple crown, racing's three biggest races—the Tour de France, Tour of Italy and the World Road Championship—all in one year, 1974. No other racer can claim *both* those achievements. The two racers who come closest are Bernard Hinault of France, who also won the Tour de France five times, and Stephen Roche of Ireland, who won the triple crown in 1987.

Longest single-day race: According to the *Guinness Book of World Records,* the longest single-day race is run from Bordeaux to Paris, France. Its distance varies with the route, but averages about 350 miles.

Fastest bicycle speed with a pace car: John Howard and his bicycle reached a speed of more than 152 miles per hour in 1985. But wait—before you run out to buy the same kind of bike he used, you ought to know how he did it. He and his bicycle were towed by a race car until he got up to about 60 miles per hour. Then the towline was cut loose, and John kept pedaling, following behind the still-speeding car. His unbelievable record could not have been set without the race car to break the wind for him. Still, few people could have ridden as fast and hard as Howard. As he approached top speed, he had to stay within *inches* of the pace car. If he fell back even slightly, he would have been caught in the car's turbulence—and probably would have crashed.

Fastest unpaced bicycle speed: The Gold Rush, a bicycle covered with an aerodynamic shell, reached 65 miles per hour on flat ground, without a pace car, in 1986. For more about the Gold Rush, see Chapter 5.

Longest distance covered by a cyclist in 24 hours on an indoor track: The record-holder is Michael Secrest, who pedaled a little more than 514 miles on the Olympic velodrome in Montreal in 1985. John Howard matched that feat outdoors when he cycled 514 miles in 24 hours around a 5-mile circuit in Central Park.

THE RACE IS ON!

Ever since the first bicycles were invented, cyclists have wanted to race. Today there are dozens of different kinds of races—everything from BMX racing on dirt tracks to high-speed track racing on tracks called velodromes. One race, the Race Across America, is 3,000 miles long but lasts only 9 days. The Tour de France, on the other hand—the most famous bicycle race in the world—is more reasonable: It covers approximately 2,500 miles in about 22 days.

Becoming a competitive racer is never easy. The pros train long and hard for these grueling races. You may not be ready for the Tour de France, but that doesn't mean you can't compete. You could even start your own bicycle competition!

THE FIRST CYCLE RACES

The year is 1795. The place is Paris. A number of young men are perched on their cycles. The cycles are called *Velociferes*, a French word meaning speed machine. But check this out: The speed machines have two wheels and a seat—and *that's all!* There are no pedals and no handlebars. The riders can't steer and they can't get up any speed.

All they can do is propel these weird machines by pushing off with their feet or running along the ground. But still the race is on!

In England cyclists raced the same machines but called them hobbyhorses. Fortunately, a man named Baron Von Drais invented handlebars as a steering device. The new machine was taken to France where they called it the *Draisienne*. Everyone raced the Draisiennes until bicycles with pedals finally arrived. Then people raced those cycles against each other and against other vehicles: horses, railroad trains and carriages.

Cycling and cycle racing were really born in France. The first pedal-driven bicycle was invented in France, and the first long-distance races took place in France, from Paris to a city named Rouen. Today, the world's most famous long-distance road race is the Tour de France.

TOUR DE FRANCE

In Europe the Tour de France is more popular than the Super Bowl is in America. The race is called a long-distance stage race because it takes place in sections or *stages*. Each day of the race is one stage, and there are 21 racing days.

The U.S. Olympic cycling team in hot competition for the 4,000-meter team pursuit.

- In the 1880s and 90s, bicycles were used by soldiers in both Europe and the United States. One company manufactured a tandem bike (built for two riders) which had a twelve-shot repeating rifle mounted on it. Other soldiers strapped their rifles to the front forks of their bikes.

Each stage of the Tour is a race from one city in France to another, around the perimeter of the entire country. Some stages of the race are mountainous. Racers must ride through the snow-capped Alps or the Pyrenees mountains. On other stages, they bounce down cobblestone streets. Each racer has five or six bikes with him. The extra bikes and a crew of about 15 people for each team, follow along with the race.

To win the Tour de France, a rider must have a lot of help from other racers. Every rider is a member of a team, and the team members all work to help the best rider on their team win. How? There are several ways. One important strategy is to help another rider by blocking the wind for him. When one cyclist is riding in front with another cyclist right behind him, it's called *drafting*. The cyclist in back doesn't have to pedal as hard to keep up, because there is less wind resistance. Team members take turns *pulling* (riding in front) for each other. Sometimes riders from different teams draft together, too. The photograph on p. 62 shows the U.S. Olympic team using state-of-the-art drafting in a race for the gold.

It's weird to watch drafting if you don't know what's really going on. It can look like one rider is trying to get ahead but can't keep up. You'll see him drop back while another rider takes the lead. You might think the rider in front is "winning," but actually it's the other way around. The cyclist in second place is going just as fast and using less energy to do it. For that reason he's really a little bit ahead in terms of being able to win.

Another racing strategy is the *breakaway*. For most of the race, the cyclists all ride together in a pack, called the *peloton* (pell-o-tahn), a French word that means lump or cluster. To win, however, the strongest cyclists must break away from the peloton. If they can leave the pack behind, they eliminate a lot of the competition. Then only the few strong riders in front have a chance to sprint forward during the final moments of each stage. No one, however, wants to ride far ahead of *all* the other riders—not until the very end, at least. Otherwise there wouldn't be anyone to help block the wind by drafting.

Although only one person can win the Tour, everyone knows that the team effort is what counts. To acknowledge the team members, many winners have chosen to give all of the prize money to the rest of the team, rather than keep it for themselves. There is one prize the winner keeps, however—a yellow jersey. Each day of the race, the cyclist with the overall best time gets to wear the yellow jersey that day. The shirt may change hands several times during the race, but only one racer has it in the end—a symbol of triumph.

Until 1986 no American had ever won the Tour de France. The best cyclists in the world were usually French or Italian. But one American cyclist, Greg LeMond, was considered to be a great rider. He was invited to join the best French team. Some people thought Greg should help the best French cyclist win. The Frenchman's name was Bernard Hinault, and he had won the Tour de France five times! Only two other cyclists had ever done that, and no one had ever won six times.

Other people, though, wanted Greg LeMond to win—including Greg himself! So, although they were supposed to be helping each other, a terrible competition flared up between Greg and Bernard. In the end, Greg won the race. It was a major victory for American cyclists and sparked a lot of interest in cycling in America. But could Greg win the Tour de France a second time? To find out, read more about Greg later in this chapter.

TOUR DE TRUMP

In May of 1989, Donald Trump, the famous billionaire real-estate developer, launched a brand-new American stage race. Called the Tour de Trump, the race lasted 10 days and covered 837 miles. Although the race covered far fewer miles than the Tour de France, the cyclists found it to be a difficult course. Starting in Albany, New York, the racers wound their way through four more states: New Jersey, Pennsylvania, Maryland and Virginia. Along the way there were various kinds of stages, including a mountain stage in upstate New York and a criterium race. (See page 65 for a description of criteriums.) During the mountain stage, some racers had to get off and walk their bicycles up the hill!

The prize money offered for the Tour de Trump totalled $250,000, with $50,000 going to Dag Otto Lauritzen of Norway, riding for the 7–eleven convenience store team, the first-place winner. His total time was 33 hours, 22 minutes and 48 seconds. Greg LeMond finished in twenty-seventh place, which shows how hard it is for even the best cyclists to win consistently.

Will the Tour de Trump become an American tradition? Only time will tell. The first year's event was a success, however, and Donald Trump always has bigger plans. In the future, he says, he might change the route so that the racers cross America, going from New York City to San Francisco or Los Angeles. Watch for it—it might even come to a city near you!

A killer mountain stage of the Tour de France.

RACE ACROSS AMERICA

Otherwise known as RAAM, this 3,000-mile race stretches from the west coast to the east coast. It's a brutal event, though, for maniac bikers only. Why? Because unlike the Tour de France, cyclists in this race don't stop to sleep eight hours each night. They sleep only two hours, then start riding again. At that pace, the best riders can finish the race in about nine days. As a matter of fact, only the best riders finish the race at all! In 1988, 33 men started RAAM but 22 of them dropped out. The women did a little better—six started the race and half of them finished.

CRITERIUM RACES

These are one-day races usually held on city streets that are blocked off for the event. The race course is a loop one or two miles long, which the riders cover over and over again. The total racing distance can be anything from 6 to 62 miles in length. Criteriums are great for spectators because if you're standing along the race course, you can see the same riders go past several times. Watch for fast action on the curves, which top-notch riders take at top speeds.

TRACK RACING

Imagine two cyclists coming to a dead stop in the middle of a race. What's happening? Are they out of breath? Are they hurt? Or are they ready to quit? None of the above. They're track-racing sprinters, and the sprint is a very strange kind of race. For one thing, the racers ride for 1,000 meters, but only the last 200 meters count. Sometimes when the race starts, the riders simply balance on their bikes, going nowhere fast! The reason is that neither of them wants to take the lead too soon, because the rider in back will benefit from drafting. It's a case of both racers saying "After you." "No, no, after *you*." "No, really, you go first and I'll follow. Really—I don't mind." Since neither rider is timed during the first 800 meters of the sprint, neither one cares how long it takes.

Track racers use specially designed high-tech bikes with no brakes and only one gear—a fast one! Their bikes are so lightweight—almost flimsy—that they would probably fall apart if

TRY IT!

Want to see how it feels to ride in someone else's slipstream? That's what the "empty" air space behind a leading cyclist is called. You can try drafting if you follow a few safety rules. First, don't try it on a busy street. Second, don't get *too* close to the lead rider. And third, be sure to stay to one side of the rider, not directly behind him or her. That way you can go around if he or she suddenly stops or falls.

Try drafting on a windy day, riding directly into the wind. You'll certainly notice the difference when it's your turn to ride in front!

ridden on a rough surface such as a concrete, potholed street. Of course, the lighter the bike, the more sophisticated the design, which means that track racers pay thousands of dollars for their skimpy machines.

The races themselves are held in special tracks or arenas called velodromes. There are only about 20 velodromes in the United States, and almost half of them are on the west coast. You probably won't see much track racing on television either, except during the Olympics.

Other track racing events are

- Time trials, in which individuals ride for 1,000 meters and the lowest time wins.
- Pursuit races, in which two cyclists start on opposite sides of the track from each other and then try to catch up with each other. If one rider overtakes the other, he/she automatically wins. Otherwise, the winner is the person with the best time.
- Points races, in which points are awarded for being ahead at certain times during the race. The winner is the racer with the most points, even if he/she doesn't cross the finish line first.

OLYMPIC BICYCLE RACING

You'll see track racing most often at the Olympics, including all of the kinds of track races mentioned

After crossing the finish line, Connie Carpenter (L) and Rebecca Twigg (R) celebrate a gold and silver finish in the 1984 U.S. Olympics.

above. There are also road races in the Olympics. In 1984 Connie Carpenter became the first American woman to win a gold medal in road racing! Not only did she take the gold in the 79-kilometer race, but her teammate, Rebecca Twigg, won the silver. The 1984 American cycling team of men and women won nine medals and helped cycling become a more popular sport.

Bicycle companies spend hundreds of thousands of dollars developing Olympic bicycles. Everything from handlebars to helmets is tested for aerodynamics. Olympic cyclists get all the hot, new equipment first. For example, disk wheels, which replaced wheels with spokes, were specially developed for the Olympics because they can slice through the air with less wind resistance or drag. (These wheels are made of two flat plates sandwiched together around a regular hub.) And carbon-fiber frames have become amazingly lightweight. Some racers' bike frames weigh only 3.3 pounds!

TRIATHLON

It sounds crazy. First you jump in the water and swim for something like half a mile. Dripping wet, you climb out and jump on your road-racing bike

WHEEL FACTS

• In 1884 an American named Thomas Stevens was the first person to bicycle around the world. He rode an Ordinary bicycle, like the one pictured on page 35. His trip took more than two years!

for 20 or 30 miles. At the end of the course, you throw down your bike and dash off to run for 15 miles or so. First one to the finish line wins!

That's a triathlon event, a race combining those three sports in that order. The idea behind it is to test an athlete's all-around fitness and endurance at the same time. If you think that's tough, how about the Ironman event in Hawaii? It's a super-triathlon which includes an ocean swim of almost 2½ miles, a bike ride of more than 100 miles and then a marathon footrace—a full 26-mile run! Get in shape before even trying to *watch* an Ironman. Just following along on the sidelines is enough to wear you out!

BMX RACING AND FREESTYLE

Here's a kind of biking competition that's custom-made for kids. In fact, kids invented BMX racing! It all began in the late 1970s when kids in California tried to use their bikes to imitate off-road motorcycle racing. They invented the wheelie and later tried to jump through the air over obstacles the way motorcyclists did. Their bikes got dented, damaged and destroyed, but a new sport was born. Pretty soon, bicycle manufacturers caught on to this and started making BMX bikes that could take the rough ride. (BMX stands for bicycle motocross—a term that comes from motorcycle cross-country racing.)

Now there are two kinds of competitions using BMX bikes—races and freestyle. BMX races are held on dirt tracks and are usually all-day events consisting of several single races called *motos*. The winners of the motos compete in one final race for the big prize—usually a trophy.

The great thing about BMX racing is that kids of all ages can compete. You don't have to be experienced. There's even a category for kids age

five and *under!* That's fairly amazing, considering that a lot of kids don't learn to ride two-wheelers until they are six years old. Kids only compete against other kids in the same age group and of the same ability. Boys and girls compete in separate races. There are beginners, novices, experts and pros. The pros, who must be at least 16 years old, can win cash prizes and are often sponsored by bicycle manufacturers.

On a BMX racetrack, there is usually a downhill section, several jumps, one or more curved sections called *berms* and a series of small bumps called "whoops" or "whoop-de-doos." Since the track is made of dirt, it can get pretty dusty.

The rules for BMX racing require that you have pads on your handlebar crossbar, the top tube, and the gooseneck (or handlebar stem). You are also required to wear a long-sleeved shirt, long pants and an extra-sturdy motorcycle-type helmet. This is *not* the kind of helmet you wear to ride a 12-speed bike. For BMXing, you'll need a helmet that surrounds your head and covers your ears. Most racers also wear special nonslip gloves and padded clothing called "leathers."

What if you want to try BMX racing, but you're not ready to go out and buy all this equipment? Don't worry about leathers. Until you get serious about the sport, a long-sleeved T-shirt and jeans will do fine. Some BMX tracks even have the necessary helmets, elbow pads and bike pads, which they will lend out for free.

More than 80,000 kids compete in BMX events each year, most of them from ages 6 to 12. The majority of kids competing own one or two seriously sturdy bikes costing $300 to $400 each.

If you'd like to find out about BMX racing in your area, you can contact the National Bicycle League or the American Bicycle Association. Their addresses are in the Appendix at the back of this book. You can also check with your local bike shop. Sometimes bike shops or organizations such as the Jaycees, Optimists, Lions Club or Kiwanis will sponsor events for kids.

BMX freestyle is a completely different kind of event. Much more dangerous than racing, freestyle competitions are scored by judges who award points for the best stunts. Freestyle stunts are performed in two ways: on curved wooden

ramps, called *quarter pipes*, and in concrete
bowls. Bowls are the kind of curved pits that were
used by skateboarders when skateboarding was
most popular. Some of the stunts are called *aerials*
because when the biker rides up the curved ramp,
he or she can become airborne for a short time.
Midair flips are common among the best riders.
BMX freestyle bikers seem to defy gravity when
they stop their bikes at the edge of a deep pit and
then turn around to ride back down the ramp
again. Helmets, elbow pads, knee pads and
leathers are essential gear in freestyle competitions.

Freestyle BMXing requires a slightly different
kind of BMX bike from the bike used in racing.
For racing, you need a strong, sturdy but
somewhat lightweight bike. The less weight, the
greater the speed. For freestyle stunts, though, you
need an even stronger, sturdier and heavier bike.
The high-impact landings that stunt riders make
can quickly pound a lighter bike into trash. BMX
freestyle bikes are also fitted with coaster brakes
instead of caliper brakes. Some of the stunts can't
be performed unless the rider can stand on the
pedals and make them "lock" into that position,
the way coaster brakes do.

AMATEUR ROAD RACING

Every Saturday morning, kids and adults all over
America compete in amateur road races
sponsored by the USCF (United States Cycling
Federation). This is the way to start if you want to
be the next Greg LeMond or Connie Carpenter!
You have to be at least 10 to enter, but there are
classes for everyone from first-timers to top-level
racers. You'll even get a racing license!

Usually these races are organized by local
cycling clubs. Your neighborhood bike shop can
put you in touch with the bike club nearest you.
Or contact the USCF, whose address and phone
number are listed in the Appendix.

Wild
competition
at your
local BMX
course!

Only a heroic effort in the time-trial stage of the 1989 Tour de France secured a victory for U.S. cyclist Greg LeMond.

WHEEL FACTS

- Since 1985 more adult bikes have been sold each year than kids' bikes. (Do you think the adults are *outgrowing* their old bikes?)

GREG LEMOND: AMERICA'S BEST SPOKESPERSON!

After winning the Tour de France in 1986, Greg LeMond was on top of the world. He was young for a cyclist—only 25 years old—and he had every reason to believe that he could win again the following year. But 1987 was not a good year for him. In the spring, he crashed and broke his wrist. Two months later he was seriously injured in a hunting accident. And then he had his appendix taken out. Greg didn't race at all that summer, so people began to wonder: Could he come back and win in 1988?

The answer was no. Greg did very well in 1988, but he didn't win the Tour. Even Greg was not surprised. He knew that his injuries had kept him from training as hard as he needed to. He even told his sponsors that he might not win until 1989.

And he was right. In 1989 Greg pedaled to victory, winning the Tour de France for a second time. In addition to his talent and training, Greg used two technical innovations to help him win. One was a real disk wheel, which was supposed to help him gain speed by streamlining the bike. Unfortunately, some parts of the racecourse were windy, and the disk wheel didn't always help. The other innovation, however, made all the difference for Greg. He rode with aerobars—handlebars that stick out over the front wheel. With aerobars, Greg was able to maintain a low, aerodynamic body position for a longer period of time.

On the final day of the race, Greg was 50 seconds behind a tough competitor—Laurent Fignon of France. Fifty seconds was a lot to make up in one day, and most people thought that even if Greg rode his best, he couldn't do it. Greg disagreed, however. He stayed completely focused on his goal, told his support crew *not* to report his times to him and concentrated on only one thing:

winning. When he finally crossed the finish line ahead of Fignon, he still didn't know whether or not he had won. The racers were actually competing against the clock, and they had begun the race that day in reverse order—with the leading cyclist starting last. Greg had to wait until Fignon crossed the finish line to find out whose time was best. In the end, Greg won the Tour by *eight* seconds. It was the sweetest victory of his career.

Greg started racing when he was 17 years old, and he truly loves cycling. He thinks he can win the Tour de France three or four times before he retires. But even if Greg never wins another road race, he has already earned his place in history as the first American to win the "race to end all races"—the Tour de France.

GLOSSARY

AEROBARS. Aerodynamically designed handlebars which point toward the front of the bike and have elbow rests.

ATB. All-Terrain Bicycle; also known as Mountain Bike.

ANKLING. Pedaling technique which helps build speed and efficiency. To ankle, toes should be pointed slightly downward at the bottom of the stroke, slightly upward at the top of the stroke.

AXLE. The shaft on which the wheel revolves.

BAR-END SHIFTER. A gear-shifting system that is operated by twisting the ends of aerobars.

BEAD. The outside edge of the tire, which is stiffened by a wire.

BINDER BOLT. Any bolt used to attach a part to a bicycle.

BMX. Abbreviation for bicycle motocross. BMX indicates a style of bike and a kind of race or competition.

BOTTOM BRACKET. The mechanism at the bottom of the bicycle frame which holds the spindle and crank.

BRAKE LEVER. A lever mounted on the handlebars to control the brakes.

BRAKE SHOE. A rubber pad which stops the bike by pressing on the tire's rim, creating friction.

CABLES. Heavy metal wires twisted into cables and sometimes covered with plastic coating. Cables are used to connect the brake levers to the brakes and to connect the gear shift levers to the derailleur.

CADENCE. The regular and rhythmic pace at which a cyclist pedals the bike.

CALIPER BRAKES. Any bicycle braking system which works by opening and closing two brake shoes on the tire's rim in a clamping motion, like jaws. Caliper brakes' hand controls are us mounted on the handlebars.

CANTILEVER BRAKES. A particular type of caliper brake suspended by a triangular cable system. Also called center-pull brakes.

CHAINSTAYS. The part of the bicycle frame that runs parallel to the chain. It connects the bottom bracket to the rear dropouts.

CHAINWHEEL. One or more large gears with teeth, located near the pedals. Also sometimes called the front gear set. The chainwheel is attached to the bottom bracket and crank.

CLICK SHIFTING. A gear shift lever that clicks into position when you've hit the right spot for each gear.

COASTER BRAKE. A brake system located inside the hub of the rear wheel and activated by pedaling backwards. Sometimes called "foot" brakes.

CRANK. The L-shaped metal arm to which the pedals are attached.

CROSSOVER BIKE. Also called a half-breed bike or city bike, this is a cycle that combines elements of both road bikes and mountain bikes.

CRUISER. Simple medium or heavyweight single-speed bicycle with coaster brakes and fenders.

CYCLOMETER. An odometer for a bicycle, measuring distance traveled.

DERAILLEUR. The mechanism which guides the chain and allows it to be shifted from one gear to another. Derailleur is a French word which means "to derail" or cause the chain to come off the rail.

DOWN TUBE. Part of the bicycle frame which slants downward at an angle. It runs from the head tube to the bottom bracket.

DROPOUTS. Small, slotted openings which hold the front and rear wheel axles. On many bikes the dropouts do not appear to be separate parts. They are merely the openings at the ends of two other frame sections: the seat stays and the front fork.

FORK. The double-pronged section of the frame which holds the front wheel.

FREESTYLE. A type of BMX bike competition involving stunt riding, usually performed on curved wooden ramps called quarterpipes.

FREEWHEEL. The set of gears or sprocket wheels attached to the rear wheel of the bike.

GEAR RATIO. A number which indicates the relationship between two gears and tells you how much work a particular combination of gears will do. To get the gear ratio, divide the number of teeth in the chainwheel by the number of teeth in the freewheel. For instance, a front sprocket with 40 teeth has twice as many teeth as a rear sprocket with 20 teeth, so the gear ratio would be 2 to 1, or simply 2. Most cyclists convert the gear ratio to gear inches by multiplying by the diameter of the rear wheel. When you know your gear ratio in inches, you'll know how each gear on your bike should be used. (See Chapter 3.)

GOOSENECK. The handlebar stem, which fits inside the head tube.

HEAD TUBE. Short vertical tube at the very front or "head" of the bike. The handlebars fit inside the head tube, and the front fork attaches to it also.

HUB. Cylinder which holds the axle of each wheel. Hubs sometimes also contain the coaster brakes and/or a simple three-speed gear shift mechanism.

MAG WHEELS. Wheels with only five large spokes molded in one single piece, rather than many wire spokes.

MOTOCROSS. Originally a cross-county motorcycle race, the term is now also used to describe BMX bike races held on dirt tracks.

ODOMETER. A device which measures the distance traveled.

PANNIERS. Pouches or saddlebags which are mounted on a bike carrier and used to carry gear.

ROAD BIKE. Lightweight bike with dropped handlebars.

SADDLE. Another name for the bicycle seat.

SEATPOST. The stem which holds the saddle and goes inside the seat tube.

SEATSTAYS. Section of the frame which runs from the seat tube to the rear wheel dropouts.

SEAT TUBE. The more or less vertical tube on the bike frame which holds the seat stem and saddle.

SEW-UPS. A kind of tire which is actually sewn around the tube. Also called tubular tires, these are used mostly for racing.

SNAKE BITES. Slang for the kind of tire puncture that occurs when an underinflated tire presses against the wheel rim.

SPROCKET. One of the teeth on a gear or cog.

TANDEM. A bicycle for two or more riders.

TIME TRIAL. A timed race in which the racers start one at a time and race against the clock. Some time trials measure the distance traveled in a set amount of time. Others measure the time it takes to cycle for a set distance.

TOE CLIPS. A small metal housing on the pedals used to strap the foot in place.

TOP TUBE. The top horizontal tube on a bicycle frame.

TOURING. Extended bicycle trips, lasting anywhere from half a day to several weeks, months or even years.

VELODROME. A track with steep banks or berms, used for bicycle track races.

More About Bicycling

You can learn a lot more about special aspects of bicycling by reading other books and contacting biking organizations. A number of excellent sources of information are listed below. Many of the organizations will send you free information if you call or write.

BIKING ORGANIZATIONS

American Bicycle Association, P.O. Box 718, Chandler, Ariz. 85244, (602) 961-1903. This organization has 65,000 members, mostly ages 5 to 25, boys and girls, who compete in BMX competitions nationwide. It costs about $25 to join, but you can get a trial membership for about $5, which will last for 30 days and even give you limited medical insurance for that time. The ABA organizes races, publishes a newsletter about BMX racing and makes the rules which govern BMX racing in America. Many of the races sponsored by the ABA are located in the western half of the United States. For information about eastern states' BMX, see the National Bicycle League.

American Youth Hostels, Inc., P.O. Box 37613, Washington, D.C. 20013-7613, (202) 783-6161. An organization that encourages bicycle touring and maintains inexpensive overnight accommodations for cyclists and hikers throughout the United States. Contact them for membership information, biking maps and tours. A youth membership costs about $10.

Bikecentennial, P.O. Box 8308, Missoula, Mont. 59807, (406) 721-1776. A good source of information about bicycle tours, along with maps and route information. The organization also publishes a magazine for members. You can get a student membership for about $19.

League of American Wheelmen, 6707 Whitestone R., Suite 209, Baltimore, Md. 21207, (301) 944-3399. This is the oldest biking organization in the U.S., which may explain why the club's name seems to exclude women (although the club itself doesn't). Contact this organization for information about local biking clubs, events and rallies. Membership, which costs about $22, includes a subscription to *Bicycle U.S.A.* magazine.

National Bicycle League, P.O. Box 729, Dublin, Ohio 43017, (614) 766-1625. A nonprofit organization with 20,000 members. The NBL organizes, promotes and sponsors BMX racing and state games. They also select the team for the BMX World Championship. Membership is about $30 for amateurs.

U.S. Cycling Federation, 1750 E. Boulder Street, Colorado Springs, Colo. 80909, (719) 578-4581. Get in touch with this organization if you want to become a competitive cyclist yourself. This group sponsors races for 10-year-olds and up. It is the governing body of amateur cycling in the United States. USCF coaches are the ones who select our Olympic cycling team. If you're 15 years old or under, membership is about $16.

RECOMMENDED BOOKS

The Complete Book of Bicycling by Eugene A. Sloane. An excellent resource, particularly good for information about technical aspects and repairs. Also includes helpful hints about biking

overseas. One of the four cyclists who toured around the world in 1981 on a special fund-raising cycle tour took a copy of this book along.

Greg LeMond's Complete Book of Bicycling by Greg LeMond and Kent Cordis. Even the most ordinary chapters of this book are interesting because they are filled with the stories of Greg's own training and racing experiences. This is a great book, but you have to remember when reading it that Greg LeMond is a professional cyclist. Some of his advice is meant for competitive athletes rather than for average kids or adults.

Richard's New Bicycle Book by Richard Ballantine. Another good, all-round resource on many aspects of cycling.

DeLong's Guide to Bicycles and Bicycling by Fred DeLong. Full of technical data and test results about bicycles and cyclists.

Bicycling: A History by Frederick Alderson. Everything you could ever want to know about the invention of the bicycle.

The Almanac. Available to members from the League of American Wheelmen, see page 76 for address. This book contains a state-by-state listing of bicycle rides and tours and bicycle clubs. Not available to nonmembers.

The Bicycle Vacations Guide. Available from Bikecentennial, address on page 76. For about $2 this guide lists 150 tour operators and includes information about trip lengths, destinations and prices.

The Cyclists' Yellow Pages. Available from Bikecentennial, address on page 76. Where to find everything connected with bike touring—hostels, biking maps, tourist information—listed in a state-by-state format.

ELECTRONIC BULLETIN BOARD

With a computer, a modem and a membership in CompuServe, you can tap into a lot of fascinating information about biking. CompuServe is an electronic information service which is accessed by computer over the telephone lines. Once you are on-line, you type the command FIND CYCLING. You will instantly be connected to the Outdoor Forum—an electronic club for people interested in all kinds of outdoor sports, including cycling. Various kinds of free software are available through the cycling section of the Outdoor Forum. You can get a program that will calculate your bicycle's gear ratios for you, or a program that will keep track of your distance traveled in a cycle training program. Or you can leave messages for other cycling enthusiasts. The forum is run by a cycling expert who will answer questions, too. For more information about CompuServe, call toll-free 1-800-848-8990.

ANSWERS TO QUIZZES AND PUZZLES

Answers to Cycle Search:

```
H  I  P  R  C  L  A  P  D  F  E  Y
E  D  E  P  I  C  O  L  E  V  A  L
B  O  N  E  S  H  A  K  E  R  S  C
G  E  N  P  R  A  I  K  G  A  F  T
U  R  Y  E  R  M  S  I  F  O  A  O
T  R  F  E  L  C  I  E  H  B  C  R
E  N  A  Q  U  A  T  O  O  R  I  D
E  S  R  O  H  Y  B  B  O  H  L  I
D  A  T  V  M  E  P  H  I  N  E  N
A  B  H  A  F  S  O  I  G  B  P  A
S  H  I  G  H  W  H  E  E  L  E  R
N  O  N  T  R  E  I  S  P  L  A  Y
I  L  G  O  U  C  R  A  Y  M  V  E
```

Answers to Trivia Match: 1B, 2C, 3E, 4D, 5A

Answers to Show-off Smart-off Quiz:
1C, 2C, 3A, 4B, 5D, 6B, 7C, 8B, 9B, 10C

PHOTOGRAPHY CREDITS

Steve Powell/Allsport: 62
Gerard Vandystadt/All-Sport: 46, 64, 70
AP/Wide World Photos: 40, 42, 45
Bruce Bennett: 68
The Bettmann Archive: 35
FPG Int'l: 40
Chris Michaels/FPG Int'l: 5
Thomas Zimmermann/FPG Int'l: 44
Diane Johnson: 57
David Madison: 43
Mary E. Messenger: 9
North Wind Picture Archives: 36, 38, 39
Greg Crisci/Photo/Nats: 4, 26
Peter Read Miller/Sports Illustrated: 66
Lane Stewart/Sports Illustrated: 30
Bob Thomas Sports Photography: 54, 58